YOU NOW HAVE HAVE CUSTODY OF YOU...

...Christian Responses to Marriage and Divorce

by
Richard M. Cromie, D.D., Ph.D.

Desert Ministries, Inc.
Matthews, North Carolina

YOU NOW HAVE CUSTODY OF YOU

First Edition
Copyright 2006 by
Desert Ministries, Inc.
P.O. Box 747
Matthews, NC 28106
ISBN 0-914733-32-X

Printed by Eagle Graphic Services, Ft. Lauderdale, FL

In Memoriam

*This book is dedicated to the memory of
Fred Courtney Babcock, a charter member of the Desert
Ministries Board of Trustees, who suggested this project
many years ago
and to Mrs. James D. (Clara) Terry,
beloved friend and benefactor of Desert Ministries.*

TABLE OF CONTENTS

ACKNOWLEDGMENTS

It has been a long journey to the publication of this book, and much has happened along the way. For one thing, the landscape of matters concerning marriage and divorce has changed and continues to change. This made the task of the writing more difficult.

I have been an active pastor in the Presbyterian Church (USA) since my ordination in 1962, and since that time, I have counseled God's children before, during and after marriage, through recovery and into second marriages and beyond. I have also been asked from time to time to share some of those experiences with young pastors in conferences and through continuing education for ministerial leaders of the faith. I published a booklet 20 years ago subtitled, In Favor of the Divorced, which is now out-of-date. In other words, I have struggled for a long time to find suitable ways to summarize some Christian reflections on marriage and divorce.

There are many people to thank along the way. The first are those who shared their ideas, fears and possibilities with me as their pastor. I have seen the worst of what people can do to torment each other. I have interceded in some dangerous and difficult family struggles. I have seen selfish motives destroy the best of people, their families and their homes.

In the process, I learned a great deal from those who confided in me during and after their struggles. Of course, I have read books galore and listened to authorities on marriage counseling. But the most valuable things I learned came from the myriad of good souls whose anonymity I will protect. There are many friends, family and parishioners who have shared with me what they were going through in deciding to marry, divorce or marry again. I thank them.

I also want to thank some individuals around me who prompted me to move along with this writing. My friend and charter board member of Desert Ministries, Inc., Fred C. Babcock, now gone, mentioned to me more than a decade ago that he would like to know what I had to say about divorce. He even funded the initial project. Clara Terry, recently deceased, kept encouraging me to finish this work, as she felt so many people need to hear a reasoned approach and attitude on the topic. God bless the memory of both of them.

Then there is my wife, Peggy Good Cromie, who kept me and my computer pounding away at the project. She has encouraged my work for more than 45 years. I will never forget the day in our first year of broadcasting sermons on the radio when Steve Zelenko, our sound engineer, came to me one day. He said with amazement that it was the first time in his career he found a preacher's wife who wanted a copy of her husband's sermon so she could listen to it again and learn more. Thanks to my Peggy.

The board members of Desert Ministries, Inc. deserve a thank-you as well. They are my friends and fellow travelers. They have been patient and supportive throughout the years. They keep me going with their prayers and participation. Bob Patton took the time to read some of the book in preparation and helped me with his comments.

Finally, there are two professional and competent friends who have excelled in their concern for what Desert Ministries is trying to do. They take our work to heart and go far beyond the call of professional duty. One is J.D. Thrower, our publisher and president of Eagle Graphic Services, in Fort Lauderdale, Florida. He has been helping me and Desert Ministries, Inc., for more than 20 years. He is a great Christian friend and fellow traveler.

The other is Holly Strawbridge, our copy editor and friend, also from Fort Lauderdale, who has helped us bring the power and peace of our materials into the lives of those who benefit from what we do. She has carefully worked through this and other books in our collection with firm counsel and patience to the end that they are worthy of publication. I am proud of and grateful for her help.

I once heard that William Faulkner said he had never actually finished a book; the time just came when he had to abandon it to the publisher. That time, long in coming, has now arrived.

PREFACE

Over the years, I have often been surprised to learn that something I view as an elementary truth is seen as a new revelation by someone else. In the personal subject we are about to cover, differences may be very pronounced. Even like-minded people who share common goals with me will not always agree on what I write.

When it comes to marriage and divorce, such differences come to the fore. Some opinions I express will no doubt offend some readers. It is unintentional. Others may applaud with gusto, but I do not seek their favor. I prefer to foster unity among people of the faith. My hope is that this book will be helpful to everyone who is interested in the subject, especially those who are, who have been or who might be considering divorce.

Divorce is dangerous ground for a pastor. No matter how carefully you try to explain your point of view, somebody will be offended by whatever reasoning you offer. Critics come in a wide variety of colors and costumes. Roman Catholic clergymen, for example, are bound by the rules and rubrics of their church. They must maintain a respectful public distance from changing attitudes on marriage, divorce and remarriage. But I have listened to the private opinions of many who lament that if they could, they would be more open to change.

In one community in which I served, we held joint pre-marital counseling sessions for members of Protestant and Roman Catholic churches. This forced us to tiptoe through certain topics and dodge questions on family planning, divorce and remarriage. The Catholic and Episcopal clergy, as well as a few others, required that the final prenuptial sessions be held separately, so they could instruct the members of their church in the particular way marriage should be conducted. Some died-in-the-wool, traditional Protestants did the same thing.

From time to time on the national and international scene we hear about prominent Roman Catholic leaders who defy Vatican directives and challenge the authority of the Roman Curia to dictate how local dioceses and parishes should respond to the changing attitudes and needs of contemporary Christians. They are usually ostracized and occasionally excommunicated from the Church.

Not only in Roman Catholicism, but in other faiths as well, there is opposition to a more liberal view of marriage and divorce. There are self appointed "defenders of the one true faith" across the Christian landscape, but largely encamped on the extreme conservative-evangelical side. They reject all attempts to be reasonable or accommodating to those who face personal difficulties in marriage, divorce and remarriage, and refuse to discuss these issues. I do not mean all conservatives and evangelicals are so rigid. I refer mainly to those who close the door on all who disagree with their literal, non-negotiable interpretations of selected New Testament verses. Rigid attitudes make it almost impossible for the divorced to seek counsel with pastors or counselors in those places. We will deal with what the Bible says about marriage and divorce in Chapter 2. You will see that some of those passages are not as definitive as they are said to be in some official doctrines.

Anyway, a broken marriage is broken, no matter how it got that way, or who was at fault. It can get worse when divorced persons seeking advice and counsel on how to begin a new life in a new marriage arrive in the House of God and are turned away. Puzzled but undaunted, these Christians-in-love are forced to move on to another pastor, or to go outside the Christian Church and be married by secular authorities.

When I was ordained into the United Presbyterian Church (now PCUSA) in the early 1960s, our pastors were not permitted to marry persons who were divorced without prior permission from a special committee of the Presbytery, our diocese. The request had to contain specific details about how the divorce or divorces came about and whether there was proper repentance shown by the applicants. I was told that the more detailed and personal the information, the more likely that the request would or would not be granted. I tried the proper procedure a few times, but I soon saw its folly. I found that breaches of confidentiality occur among church administrators, and the bias of those who made decisions could be influenced.

For example, one senior committee member telephoned me one day to say that I did not have the correct information on one of my petitions. He had received a call from the former wife of the man who had asked me to officiate at his new marriage. With her obviously personal bias, she told the committee member "what really happened."

Meanwhile, I had met with the couple requesting marriage and had first-hand information. I was troubled. I appealed to my senior pastor, who told me that if I felt led to perform the marriage in the presence of God, I should do it. I did. However, the issue has not gone away in all 45 years of my ministry.

In the last decade of my active work, I was called to be pastor of The Royal Poinciana Chapel in Palm Beach, Florida. This interdenominational house of God had more than a century of exceptional ministry. While retaining my Presbyterian ordination, I was pleased to be able to welcome people of all faiths to worship and to be available for weddings, funerals and other rites for many who had been turned away by other congregations.

At the Chapel, we struggled continually with how to remain a Christian Church and not become a Las Vegas-type of drive-through wedding establishment. We probably made some mistakes, but it was worth the risk. The compassion we were able to show to those who had been divorced was literally a Godsend that gave them a head start on their new lives. As witness to that, many of those we first met on a wedding application became and remained active members of the Chapel or are now devoted members of other Christian churches.

Beyond the churches that make it difficult to approach marriage and divorce fairly, I am aware of those who are caught up in the changing ethos of our modern world, those who have removed themselves completely from the theological-moral dynamics of our topic. We live in a post-modernist secular climate. There is a routine assumption that the articles of our faith and the teachings of the Bible are no longer relevant to contemporary social and ethical issues. Proponents of that stance urge us on to a more rational life, unencumbered by what an ancient religious book means or does not mean to our contemporary world. These critics have moved marriage to an optional choice as convenience dictates. It reminds me of that famous cartoon in which a liberal young justice of the peace asks the couple standing before him, "John, will you take Mary to be your lawfully wedded wife, so long as it is convenient for both of you?"

We have been told that "living together" is acceptable, as least for as long as it is convenient. Advocates say it is just as good as marriage and maybe better. If the arrangement does not work out, the partners simply say goodbye. We often read or hear advice that it is better not to marry at all. Sometimes it is disguised as the convenience of living together to share expenses and common chores. Or it is said that a trial-run to decide whether marriage will work is a good idea. Or it enables couples to be together without family and economic consequences, or a multitude of other reasons.

I admit that I have seen some instances where any one of the above reasons appeared to be sensible. But when taken out of individual context, all of them are an assault on the institution of marriage.

Some of my academic friends wonder why I continue to focus on what the Bible says and means. They tease that I am a slave to some selected ancient words and irrelevant customs. I think not. I believe the Bible is the revealed Word of God, given to help us find our way in a milieu that lacks direction. I refuse to discard the Scriptures as an out-of-date document. I am not a Biblical literalist, but I still insist that we wrestle with the words of the text, even though translations can be misleading. There have been inaccuracies in translations, mistakes and interpolations by copyists. There are some isolated cases where the original text was so unclear that an arbitrary declaration of how it should be translated and interpreted was necessary. There are a myriad of situations in which the meaning of words has changed from the time the Scriptures were written. For detailed information on this subject, I recommend a new book by Professor Bart Ehrman at the University of North Carolina called, Misquoting Jesus.

If the Bible is not the Word of the Lord, then it really does not matter how we proceed. But since in the tradition of our faith, we believe the 66 books of the Old and New Testaments are the Word of God for his people, then we need to read and listen carefully, or we will overlook the grace and guidance that we need. A proper hermeneutic (our method of interpreting the meaning of the Bible) requires that we search in and around the English translations of the original words. When these are in place, we can all happily state, "This is the Word of the Lord!" The response is, "Thanks be to God!"

CHAPTER 1
TIME AND CHANGE, MARRIAGE AND DIVORCE

Marriage and divorce are the primary concerns of this book, but they occur in the larger context of our lives. Change is constant, especially in the way the acceptance of divorce has been emerging over the past several decades.

The experiences of the British Royal Family since I was born provide an excellent illustration. When King George V died in 1936, Edward VIII ascended to the throne. However, Edward had become infatuated with an American divorcée named Wallis Simpson. Following his coronation, he announced that he wanted to marry her. The trouble was that Wallis was still married to her second husband, Ernest Simpson. Technically, she was the mistress of the new king.

There was no official or legal impediment to their marriage, but a furor followed as the Anglican Church, the Royal Family and the British Government objected. Edward was torn between the woman he loved and his kingdom. He decided in favor of the woman, and abdicated his throne. He and Wallis were married six months later. Not one member of the Royal Family attended the wedding.

In the next generation Princess Margaret, the younger sister of Queen Elizabeth II, fell in love with Captain Peter Townsend. They wanted to marry, but Townsend was divorced. The mores of the time made the intended marriage inadvisable. Margaret was heartbroken. In 1955, she announced she would not marry the captain. She said "she was mindful of the Church's teaching on marriage and divorce and of her duty to the Commonwealth." Margaret eventually married Lord Anthony Snowden. When they were divorced in 1978, it was the first Royal divorce in Great Britain since Henry VIII in the 16th century.

Finally, we come to the recent marriage of Charles, Prince of Wales, to Camilla Parker Bowles. Prince Charles had married Diana Spencer in 1981. They were already divorced when Princess Diana died in a car accident in 1997. Camilla was divorced from Andrew Parker-Bowles in 1995. Charles, the heir to the throne, admitted publicly that he and Camilla were "romantically involved" even during the time he and Diana were married.

On April 9, 2005, Charles and Camilla were married in a civil ceremony with much fanfare and little criticism. Their union received the blessing of the Anglican Church in St. George's Chapel at Windsor Castle later in the day. Members of the Royal Family joined in the blessing and attended the reception that followed. The whole spectacle caused a big headache for Queen Elizabeth, but you can imagine what her Uncle Edward would have said.

My purpose is not to tarnish the reputation of the British monarchy, but to illustrate how our attitudes change. The acceptance of infidelities and divorce in the Royal Family mirrors what has happened in our society. The world is not the same as it was one generation ago. The moral and ethical absolutes demanded at that time have been replaced by tolerance and acceptance.

The world is not a perfect place. Times are dangerous and difficult. Hearts ache and break. Wars, disease and accidents crush the finest and the strongest among us. Children are frequently shortchanged. Mental-emotional diseases devastate families and society. Our selfish expectations get the best of us, and family life and marriages get the worst of it. The world is out-of-joint.

The entire marriage landscape is also out-of-whack. This is not how it should be. Marital problems abound, partly due to our demand for instant pleasure. About half of all American marriages end in divorce. Many of those could have been avoided with proper care and preparation. Each one represents a broken dream. Serial marriages are commonplace. The number of those who play at marriage by living together without benefit of nuptials is rising strikingly.

I, as many others, wonder why and how it came to be this way. The more important question is, what we can do about it before it is too late?

A primary reason for writing this book is to share my study of what the Bible says about divorce, a subject explored in depth in our next chapter. The author of Ecclesiastes wrote, "There is a time for everything under the sun" (Ecclesiastes 3). Once you understand what he meant and place it in the larger context of God's will, you can feel safe and secure, however steep and rugged your journey may be. If you focus on the life you have been given as a gift from God, you can catch hold of yourself, anchor yourself to the pillars of faith, hunker down as best you can and keep on keeping on. To do this, you need to take charge of you.

There you have it, the whole point and purpose of this book in a nutshell: you now have custody of you. Wherever you are, or have been or are planning to go, be sure you have claimed full custody of you before you continue your journey. If you are single or single-again, married or married-again, or if you are in a special relationship that crosses traditional boundaries and expectations, it does not matter. You have one life to live, so make sure you live it with all the grace and gusto you can!

A marriage does not always work out the way it should. Only a scoundrel would stand at the altar thinking about the day divorce will end it. Times change and things happen. Problems you heard about but never expected to face set up shop on your doorstep. It's not always fair—but then, the Creator God never promised that life would be fair. To wonder why things happen as they do is our eternal lot. The Scriptures often struggle with that query. The author of the book of Ecclesiastes, tries to explain it by saying, "Again I saw that under the sun the race is not to the swift, nor the battle to the strong, nor bread to the wise, nor riches to the intelligent, nor favor to the men of skill; but time and chance happen to them all" (Ecclesiastes 9:11). It comes down to the fact that bad things do happen to good people. The rain falls everywhere.

Years ago, after a particularly difficult round in the British Open at Muirfield, someone asked Jack Nicklaus if he thought the golf course had been fair to the golfers that day. The rough was as high as an elephant's eye, and the wind and rain had beat against the players all day long. Nicklaus thought about the question for a minute and responded, "I never thought that it was intended to be fair, I thought it was intended to be difficult." He was referring to golf, but I add that it also describes the passing days and decades of our lives.

Most of us start out assuming that we are entitled to smooth and easy going over the three score and 10 years we are promised in the Scripture. The Psalmist goes on to say: "Yet is their strength labor and sorrow; for they are soon cut off and we fly away." (Psalm 90:10). Years ago I had a friend who told me in his lingering terminal illness, "Until they do to me what they did to Jesus, I have no right or reason to complain," and he didn't.

Jesus reminded us in the Sermon on the Mount that the Heavenly Father makes the sun "rise on the evil and on the good, and sends rain on the just and unjust alike" (Matthew 5:45). The Lord set the framework so that we would not work too hard trying to figure it all out. We are entitled to ask why over and over, but even the Bible admits that at times "the heavens are silent."

We need to be reassured that Christ will see us through, as he promised. The road can be rugged and steep, but he is a wonderful guide. God knows our mortal frame. He remembers that we belong to him. He looks out for us as parents watch out for their children. Even the hairs of our heads are numbered. He notices it when one small sparrow falls to the earth (Matthew 10:29). The One who made the starry heavens knows each of us by name. That is an honor worth remembering. You matter to the Lord God. No matter what happens to you, his concern for you will never change. He will not fail you nor forsake you.

The process of creation was not for naught. The Garden of Eden was given to Adam and Eve. They also were given dominion over the fish in the sea, the birds in the air and every other living thing. The plants and animals belonged to them as well. They had each other, too. The one restriction was that they were not to touch the Tree of the Knowledge of Good and Evil. But being free spirits, they were not long in challenging the command of God. They took of the tree. God was angry. Adam and Eve hid. They thought the Lord would not be able to find them.

When God asked them what happened, Adam blamed Eve, and Eve blamed the serpent. The Lord God blamed both of them. The first couple of the Earth had violated a sacred trust. They were punished, along with the serpent. The snake lost his legs. Eve lost her equality. Adam was forced to earn a living by the sweat of his brow. It would be toil and trouble, penury and woe for Adam and his descendants forever.

While the "forbidden fruit" of sexual contact is suspiciously connected to what happened in the Garden of Eden, the meaning is not clear. The more important event was the couple's disobedience to God. Eve and Adam wanted to gain the knowledge of good and evil and move closer to the province of God.

Forty years ago I wrote my doctoral thesis on the relationship of the creation of man and woman to Christian theology and ethics. I discovered a wide variety of interpretations of these Genesis passages. I was astonished to learn that the Jewish scholars who studied the Old Testament through the centuries were not overly concerned with Adam's and Eve's misdeed; neither were they impressed with the Christian concept of Original Sin. They do not share the literal reading of the creation stories.

The Old Testament Jewish Scriptures that follow Genesis do not dwell on the idea, either. It is barely mentioned. Original Sin is a Christian interpretation of Genesis. Jewish theology has never taught that the sin of the first man somehow tainted each and every member of the human race that follows. In the Jewish tradition, the early stories in Genesis are symbolic, as they are with many Christians.

The Doctrine of Original Sin developed as a quintessential teaching of traditional Christian theology, primarily in the New Testament Epistles of St. Paul. Christian theology teaches that the death of Jesus of Nazareth was the means God used to reconcile his alienated children and bring them back to a new Eden. In order to accomplish it, God's only Son had to pay the price of sin by suffering and dying on the cross.

It is imperative that the enormity of the Original Sin be of such magnitude that it would require nothing less than the sacrifice of God's perfectly obedient son to assuage its power. It is also imperative that the sin of Adam be inherited by every child born until the end of time. Each must be involved in the inheritance of imperfection. The only human who escaped was Jesus of Nazareth, the sinless Son of God. Traditional Theology of Atonement requires that every other man, woman and child is in need of redemption. The sin that causes our separation from the Creator is not our day-to-day sins and peccadilloes, but that which comes as an inherent part of our being.

In my doctoral research, I introduced the theoretical question of what might have happened if the original sin of Adam and Eve had never been committed. I came to the conclusion that if the first couple had obeyed God and never touched the tree, the sacrificial death of Jesus Christ would never have been required. They were told they would die if they touched the tree, so it can be assumed that they would not have died had they obeyed the Lord and left the tree alone. Presumably, they would have lived in the Garden of Eden forever.

Whatever happened with the forbidden tree in the Genesis story, it was at least a stupid and selfish thing for Adam and Eve to have done. God was obviously troubled when they ignored his command, even if the promised punishment that they would die instantly was not carried out. They survived and lived on, but they paid a severe price. Their worst punishment was banishment from the Garden forever. As a consequence, joy and peace are not our daily fare. We, too, have been driven out.

My point in introducing this background from Genesis and creation is to share the context in which this book is written. I believe in the love God has for all his children and the love they all can have for each other. In order to understand marriage and separation, we need to set some framework about how human relationships first began.

While I do not hold to a strict literal interpretation of the words of the Bible, I believe the Scriptures are the source of our Christian faith and practice. Whether one believes in the verbal-plenary inspiration of the Scriptures – that is, each word was dictated by God—or whether one regards these stories as ancient attempts to discover the meaning of the universe or any option in between, the meaning and message remain the same.

To wit, our lives were created for a purpose. You and I did not arrive on the earth by chance. Since we were made in the image and likeness of the Creator God, we did not just happen one day. We were delivered by the One Eternal God to a specific time and place. Even the least among us has a God-given purpose to fulfill.

The days and decades of our lives have meaning, time and space notwithstanding. We all have gifts and carry in our make-up a piece of the eternal puzzle. Robert Browning used to say that life has its purpose: "To find it is your meat and drink." The Lord God is happy you are here. You arrived on earth not when you chose, but when the Lord had need of you. So long as the Lord God continues to have that need, nothing you are or do will fall outside his care and keeping. It does not matter if you are married or single or divorced.

Jesus told us that there will be no marriages in heaven. Our existence in eternity, so far as we are told in the Bible, will transcend the connections we make with each other here on earth. In the presence of God, all other relationships pale in importance. A thousand years pass like a watch in the night.

We each have a proper place to find on earth and a specific purpose to fulfill. What you choose to do about it remains your personal choice. You certainly have full custody of that. You are in charge of you. You can decide what you want to do. We do not control what happens when the rains begin to fall, but we can control what we make of it. You have sole possession of how you intend to navigate your passages. You must love, honor and obey yourself, as you love, honor and obey the Lord God who gave you life.

Having custody of you means you must take charge of your own gifts, possibilities and circumstances. The Lord God expects it. To do so properly, you must attach yourself to something enduring beyond your present predicament. Whitman once wrote that, "The finger of the whole universe is pointing unerringly in one direction, namely to you." That sounds formidable when you first hear it and realize what it means, but if you work at it, it will soon become a sacred obligation, a certain joy and an everlasting friend.

I encourage you to keep these opening thoughts in your mind, heart and soul as we proceed. If you have been badly shaken by a divorce and feel betrayed and victimized, you should not forsake yourself. Robert Frost once wrote a simple poem about a windstorm that blew down a huge tree on the road to his New England farmhouse. It took a long time to remove the debris, piece by piece, but the inconvenience was temporary. Before long, the last log was removed, and the roadway was opened again.

It is more fun to have someone to share your time with, but you can manage on your own if you decide to or are forced to. You are not a puppet on a string doing someone else's bidding. You are a child of God, an original creation, with all the rights and privileges which accompany that vaunted status. You have freedoms galore to use as you please.

The second chapter of I Peter provides a fitting summary:

"You are a chosen people...God's own people
so that you may declare the wonderful deeds
of him who called you out of darkness into his
marvelous light" (I Peter 2:9).

So, as we were taught to do when we receive a gift, we say "Thank You." Even if you do not want or need what you were given, you can pretend to like it. Say, "Thank you Lord. Now turn me loose and watch me go."

CHAPTER 2
WHAT THE BIBLE SAYS ABOUT DIVORCE

This chapter is for men and women who look to the Word of God for help in making moral decisions and who want to know what the Bible says about divorce. The wide variety of comments and situations the Scriptures offer can be confusing. The issue is not as clear as some try to make it. Far too much frustration, tension and heartbreak have resulted from the arbitrary ecclesiastical dictates resulting from these passages. I will take you through the Bible and discuss a selected sample of relevant passages in both Testaments to help answer the question of what the Bible really says and means.

Genesis 1 and 2

In the opening chapter of Genesis, the Creator makes man and woman after his likeness: "in the image of God he created him; male and female he created them." They were given dominion over all the creatures of the earth. God blessed them and told them to be fruitful and multiply and to fill the earth with people (Genesis 1:27-28).

In Genesis 2, which was apparently written by a different author, the story takes a slightly different slant. Here, man was created first to take care of the Garden of Eden. He got to name all the animals and birds. But all the birds, fish, animals and insects in the world were not enough to make him happy. He was lonely. So God put him to sleep and formed a woman from one of his ribs. The man was pleased with his new helper.

These are interesting passages, to be sure. Genesis 2:24 is normally used to teach the origin and sanctity of marriage. Expositors of the Bible have long taught that God made Adam and Eve for each other; or to be more technical, the Creator made Eve for Adam. What's more, to stretch the point, it has been taught that the Creator intended them to be married and to stay together for life: "Therefore, a man leaves his father and mother and cleaves to his wife."

Many Biblical commentators say this passage shows the original order of creation: God's intention that men and women would marry and mate each other. I obviously affirm the goodness of marriage, but if the Creator commanded every man on earth to be married to one wife for life, then divorce and any other lifestyle that men and women might choose would be automatically opposed to the original purpose of God.

The ensuing Old Testament books show how God's people played out that concept through many generations. Marriage was a sacred duty to the Israelites. A man could remain unmarried only if he chose to devote his entire life to the study of religious law (the Torah). It was customary for all young Jews to marry, usually as arranged by their parents. From what we know, many of the prophets, judges, priests and religious leaders had wives. In the time of Jesus, the Pharisees were still required to marry. It can be assumed that as healthy young Jewish men, the 12 disciples would also have been married. We do know that Jesus healed the mother-in-law of Simon Peter, the Rock on whom Jesus built his Church.

Yet on closer look, Genesis 2:24 does not say that a man and a woman were meant to be married to each other for life. There is no stated requirement that a man and a woman must be married to fulfill the purposes of God. When the chapter ends, there is still an option to marry. No wedding is mentioned in the text. It was too early in the social and religious development of the Jewish community for formal marriage ceremonies and receptions. The union was sealed in a covenant, or a contract, sometimes in writing, sometimes not. It was an agreement between two families, not a legal act in the community.

The passage was likely written at a later time. Eve is referred to as Adam's wife, but that would have little meaning in the Garden of Eden story. The main emphasis was not on marriage, but on the attraction the lonely man had for the woman. We read, "Therefore a man leaves his father and his mother and cleaves to his wife, and they become one flesh. And the man and his wife were both naked, and were not ashamed" (Genesis 2:24-25). To underscore the symbolic nature of the passage, we know it refers to Adam and Eve, but neither had a father or mother in Eden from which they could depart.

Subsequent developments in the Old Testament, as we point out elsewhere in this book, reveal a wide diversity of relationships between men and women. Universal marriage of one man to one woman was not the primary end for the chosen people of God. The Torah is clear that divorce was not only permissible; it was an easy process, especially for the man. Moses allowed that a certificate of divorce could be given to the wife by the husband and that he could send her away for a just cause, or simply at his bidding.

Multiple marriages and polygamy were well-known. Abraham, Jacob, Elkanah, Samson and many others had more than one wife. II Samuel 5 tells how King David, who already had several wives, "took more concubines and wives from Jerusalem." I Kings 11:3 relates the astounding total for Solomon; "seven hundred wives, princesses, and three hundred concubines."

In the New Testament, the words from Genesis 2 are often quoted as an indication of the centrality of marriage in the time and providence of God. Jesus even uses an adaptation of the words in Mark 10 (We will return to that passage later in this chapter). Suffice it to notice that Jesus explains that Moses allowed for a certificate of divorce because of "their hardness of heart."

In other words, the ethos changed after Adam and Eve were driven out of Eden. If it were the original intent of God for every man to be married to one woman forever, times had surely changed. After all, Jesus was forever single.

In Ephesians 5, St. Paul wrote, "Husbands should love their wives as they love their own bodies." And, "For this reason a man shall leave his father and his mother and shall be joined to his wife, and the two shall become one flesh." He adds that the marriage itself and the assumed superiority of the husband are profound mysteries.

One thing is certain: St. Paul could not be using Genesis 2:24 as proof that the original order of creation is for every man to be married to a woman, for almost in the same breath, he encourages his fellow Christians to remain single, "as I am." He apparently shared life-long bachelorhood with his Master. Some have argued that as a Pharisee Paul of Tarsus would have been married, for marriage was required in order to become a Pharisee. But we must set aside that argument for the moment. (For more information read, Was Jesus Married?, by William E. Phipps: Harper and Row, New York, 1970).

To summarize the Scriptural references from Genesis 1 and 2, the authors were relating the origin of creation. They wanted everyone to know that God made the world. It was imperative that this be stated at the start, because other cosmologies were prevalent in the writers' day. The Zoroastrians, for example, taught that two equally powerful gods were vying with each other for control of the universe. Greek and Roman mythologies repeat that scenario much later.

The Scripture writers believed that the eternal warfare between good and evil was already over. There was no question in Genesis of how the world came to be. It did not arrive by its own power, as other creation stories were saying, but it was created with purpose by the one true Creator God.

The second thing Genesis believed was that God had created human beings with a purpose. They did not arrive of their own volition or by accident. The Creator breathed his own life into them, and they became not only living beings, but the children of God. In that era it was commonplace to believe that man was superior to woman. We conclude that Genesis 2:24 was written not so much to make marriage the universal norm, but to ensure that the man (or woman) who chose to be married would leave their childhood home and the control of their parents and be bound together as one flesh.

Exodus 21:10

This brief passage introduces the requirement that a man who marries a second wife must still take care of the wife he has dismissed. The setting actually refers to a woman who was sold into slavery and subsequently married, then divorced. Surely the fulfillment of the marriage contract to provide food, clothing and security to an abandoned slave girl could be easily upgraded to provide for a free wife who is sent out on her own. The verse reads, "If he takes another wife to himself, he shall not diminish her food, her clothing, or her marital rights." (The "her" refers to the divorced wife who had been a slave). Even then, the former husband was still responsible for the continued well-being of the woman he turned loose, unless and until she married another.

I do not imply that a divorced man must continue to take care of his ex-wife for all her days. However, on a voluntary basis, or on a decision from the court, the husband is obligated to provide for his wife and their children, if applicable, in her life beyond her marriage to him. In our day it could well be the wife who should provide for the husband, depending on the circumstances. The responsibility can be fulfilled by a one-time settlement or by regularly scheduled payments, but responsibility for the spouse, or their children, does not end when the other decides to abandon the marriage.

The purpose of including the Exodus passage is to show that divorce was so common an occurrence in the Jewish community that a set of laws provided for amicable settlements of financial responsibilities, even when the wife was in bondage.

Ezra 10: 2-5, 6-19

This is a little-known and seldom-used passage of Scripture, but it touches an important aspect of our argument. Throughout the Old Testament, the chosen people were warned not to marry foreign women from outside the Jewish faith, a warning that has lingered on over the centuries and is still echoed by parents and clergy. But it happens anyway, as it did in ancient times. In this case, while the people of God were exiled in Babylonia, many Israelite men married foreign women who worshiped alien gods. When they returned, Ezra told them they had violated the command of God.

What follows is germane to what the Bible says about marriage and divorce. Ezra wept and cast himself down on the ground, telling them they had broken their pact with God in marrying these foreign women. He added that there could still be hope for the Israelites in spite of their transgressions: "Therefore, let us make a covenant with our God to put away all these wives and their children.... be strong and do it." It turned out that so many men had brought their Babylonian wives back with them that it took three full months to conduct the necessary hearings one by one. When it was all over, they abandoned their wives and children, obliterating the bonds of marriage for no cause other than that the wives were of foreign birth. In Ezra's thinking, they did not belong to the returning community of God's chosen people.

I include this passage not to praise or condemn Ezra and his fellow leaders, although I have my opinion. I selected it to show that under particular circumstances divorce on a massive scale was not only allowed, but was forced on the children of God. Genesis implied that marriage is sacred, but apparently it did not apply to marriage with foreign women.

Hosea 1 ff

Hosea loved his wife, Gomer. No matter what she did, he would not let her go. She ran off with other men, making a complete fool of her husband, but when she returned, Hosea took her in again. His neighbors warned that she was using him and wondered why. "Because I love her," was all Hosea could say.

The point of his prophecy is that God also loves his chosen people in the same way. No matter what they do, or how many times they turn their backs on his commandments, the Creator God will not forsake them. "When Israel was a child, I loved him, and out of Egypt I called my son. The more I called them, the more they went away" (Hosea 11:1-2). "They shall return and dwell beneath my shadow; they shall flourish like a garden...." (Hosea 14:7). The message in Hosea teaches the everlasting love of God for his people, as if the Creator God were the husband, and the people of the nation were his corporate bride.

There are several other instances in the Old Testament where God refers to himself as the husband of Israel, and the nation is the "bride of Yahweh." Jeremiah uses the marriage analogy for God's relationship to his chosen (Jeremiah: 3:14). Isaiah refers to the nation of Israel as "the bride of His youth" (Isaiah 54:5-6). Ezekiel declares the nation was faithless to her bridegroom, for "she went off and played the harlot with her lustful neighbors" (Ezekiel 16: 23-26).

Infidelity was familiar to the people, as was the pain it

causes, whether it was a husband, a wife or the Lord who was forsaken. Hosea was not interested in marriage and its consequences, but in the way his love for Gomer reflected the Love of God for his people. His prophecy is the paramount example of the faithfulness of God. "We love because he first loved us" (I John 4:19). I include Hosea in our study to call attention to the fact that both marriage and divorce were present, as were forgiveness and restoration.

Malachi 2: 13-16

The last book of the Old Testament features a series of arguments or complaints that God had with his people, "in your offerings, in your faithlessness, in corrupting the covenant."

In 2:13-16, Malachi turns his attention to marriage and divorce, saying that God will no longer accept their offerings with favor, "because the Lord was witness to the covenant between you and the bride of your youth, to whom you have been faithless, though she is your companion and your wife by covenant." "For I hate divorce, says the Lord the God of Israel…. So take heed to yourselves and do not be faithless."

Many reputable students and exegetes of the scripture inform us that the exact meaning and context of the Hebrew words translated as, "I hate divorce," are uncertain. However, we are prepared to take them more or less at face value. There are other passages of Scripture that teach a man should be faithful to the bride of his youth. The same is true with wives and their husbands. All who enter the marriage covenant have the same responsibility. It should be clear from our discussion of Hosea that God does not condone infidelity and divorce.

When Malachi says that God hates divorce, he declares an uncompromising reminder that however open we want to be about the subject, and however kind we are to those who have been abused, ignored or threatened by a spouse, God would prefer it if divorce never occurred at all. God is supremely disappointed with the way things turn out with His children, and it grieves Him to his heart. The earth and its inhabitants were so corrupt at the time of Noah that the Lord brought an end to every human being on earth, except for the righteous Noah and his family.

In our time it is fair to guess that God is unhappy with much of what we do and allow in our lives. To say he hates corruption and war and hunger and homelessness and starving children and abusive husbands and greedy wives and thoughtless parents, etc., is obviously true. Divorce is harmful to the equilibrium of God's children. It would be hard to find anyone who does not hate divorce, especially if they have been through a difficult separation.

But notice what God particularly hates: Malachi says God hates the unfaithfulness that caused the hurt, separation and divorce. He does not refer to proceedings in a divorce court or to the haggling over property or custody of children. We live outside Eden, and we are not yet home to paradise. In the meantime, we must make due as best we can. The words of God in Malachi are no doubt correct: divorce is a compromise between what should be and would be. If sin and selfishness did not control our day-to-day lives, there would be no need for divorce and separation.

Deuteronomy 24:1-4

No study of what the Bible says about divorce can

ignore these verses taken from the Torah. This is the lode-stone. I saved this Old Testament teaching until last, because its content transitions directly to our study of the New Testament. The verses read:

> *"When a man takes a wife and marries her, if then she finds no favor in his eyes because he has found some indecency in her, and he writes her a bill of divorce and puts it in her hands and sends her out of his house, and she departs out of his house, and if she goes and becomes another man's wife, and the latter husband dislikes her and writes her a bill of divorce and puts it in her hands and sends her out of his house, or if the latter husband dies, who took her to be his wife, then her former husband, who sent her away, may not take her again, after she has been defiled; for this is an abomination before the Lord."*

This passage is often mentioned in the New Testament. These are the verses that Jesus was reinterpreting in his argument with the Pharisees over whether or not a man can lawfully divorce his wife. We will delay some of our discussion on their meaning until we come to the parallel Gospel passages. At this point, we note that Deuteronomic Law obviously permitted divorce. The Torah is the word of the Lord to Jews and Christians alike. Notice that it omits the privilege of the wife to issue a bill of divorce to her husband. And, curiously, it declares against the right of two persons to be married a second time to each other. As the passage develops, this last item is blown out of proportion.

The verses in Deuteronomy articulate the right of the

husband to send his wife away, "if she finds no favor in his sight because of some indecency" (the first husband's sight, that is). From a literal reading of the text, it appears the second husband could send her away simply because he disliked her.

There is a wide variety of commentary available on what "indecency" might allow him to divorce her. The Old Testament Hebrew word for "indecency" and its New Testament Greek counterpart "porneia" are often translated "adultery," "immorality" or "unchastity." That would seem to be quite specific and in line with the classical interpretation of the text, which states that no other ground for divorce is permissible. But as it turns out, the phrase is not so clear.

In the centuries before Jesus, a difference of opinion had developed between two schools of thought. The School of Hillel, named for the famous Rabbi of that name, interpreted the "except for indecency" phrase as allowing divorce for almost any reason at all. It says "if she lost favor in his eyes," he could divorce her, even for something as simple as spoiling his evening meal.

The School of Shammai, which was equally prominent among the Pharisees at the time of Jesus, took a narrower view of Deuteronomy 24. While the Hillelites emphasized the part of the law that says, "If he found no favor in her" and, subsequently, that divorce could be initiated by the husband for almost any reason at all, the Shammaites shifted attention to the second part of the verse. They interpreted "indecency in the wife" to mean that divorce was permissible only if a literal sexual indiscretion had taken place. They confined the admissible evidence to offenses such as adultery, unchastity and serious sexual deviation outside the marriage. Only then could the husband dismiss his wife. If the husband were guilty of these offenses, the wife usually had no choice but to bear the hurt.

It is imperative that we appreciate the nuances of that continuing debate in order to understand how Jesus responded to the challenge from the Pharisees recorded in Matthew 19 and Mark 10. Jesus appears to be much closer to the School of Shammai. He was not intentionally taking their side; he was defending a stringent application of the law to counteract the prevalence of casual divorces in his day.

In the 1st century C.E., husbands could find or manufacture any cause they chose to dismiss their wives. Divorce of the no-fault variety was even more prevalent among the Jews and the Romans of the time than it is today in our permissive culture. It seems as though the Jewish community subscribed to the Roman custom. We will continue this discussion later in the Gospel passages, but to conclude here, Jesus elevated his response over and above their petty disputes and returned their attention to marriage and divorce in their original setting in Genesis.

The Gospels: Matthew 5: 31-32; Matthew 19: 3-12; Mark 10: 2-12; and Luke 16:18.

I copy these passages from the Gospels later in this section, but they, and the ones found in the Epistles of St. Paul, are the backdrop for what is arguably the most vigorous and volatile disagreement of interpretation in all that Jesus taught. Divorce and remarriage head the list. The battle lines between Roman Catholic and Protestant were formed as far back as the Reformation in the 16th century—perhaps earlier. From then and up through the 21st century, they have generated more comment and reflection and writings than all the other synoptic problems put together.

There are otherwise perfectly sane scholars, pastors, priests, laymen and entire Christian denominations who use these Gospel passages to teach that Jesus did not allow divorce or remarriage. A marriage was forever sacred. Augustine later added "sacramental," using the same word that belongs to the sacraments of Holy Communion, ordination and baptism. The only way a marriage could end and a divorced person marry another would be for the marriage never to have taken place. That translates to having the first marriage obliterated before another marriage could be blessed. Annulment means that the marriage never occurred, even though proper vows were spoken, Church and State officials endorsed it, and signed marriage certificates confirmed it in writing.

I need to watch my bias. I am an ordained Presbyterian pastor. I do not want to offend fellow clergy, professors, teachers or friends, who disagree with me, but I have no choice. There has been some loosening of earlier attitudes in recent decades, but the basic teaching remains the same.

I take a risk in being honest even if it offends, because I have been present in countless heartbreaking situations where two people were in love, but they could not be married in their church. They were told that if they were married any place else by anyone else, they would be living in sin. I have heard ad infinitum about how a church denomination would not permit a marriage to take place unless and until some parochial idiosyncrasies were religiously followed. I have had to try to explain ad nauseam why a

Christian priest or pastor would not marry a couple because one or both of them had been divorced, even if they were not at fault. I have heard the words, "That's what the Bible says, there is nothing I can do about it!" too many times. I have witnessed broken families, strained marriages and bewildered children as a result of the way the words of Jesus were interpreted.

The actual teaching of Jesus in his Sermon on the Mount begins with a brief introduction to marriage and divorce. The passage arises in a series of antitheses that follow the Beatitudes in which Jesus updates some ancient laws. Each set begins with the preface, "You have heard that it was said to the men of old…but I say to you…." For example, Matthew 5:21-22 reads, "You have heard that it was said… 'You shall not kill,' …but I say to you that everyone who is angry with his brother shall be liable to judgment…and whoever says 'You fool!' shall be liable to the hell of fire." Those are extreme statements that most Christian believers would be reluctant to take literally and impose on another person. No sensible person would condone a law that says, "If you call another person a fool, you will burn in the fires of hell."

Matthew 5: 27-28 goes on to say, "You have heard that it was said, 'You shall not commit adultery.' But I say to you that everyone who looks at a woman lustfully has already committed adultery with her in his heart." Again, this extreme statement from Jesus is obviously not intended to be taken literally. In that day, adultery was punishable by death. If lust were the equivalent of adultery, then looking at a woman with desire would have been a capital offense as well.

I do not believe these statements were to be taken at face value. They were spoken in hyperbole, a style that Jesus used at other times. For example, he said, "It is easier for a camel to go through the eye of a needle than for a rich man to enter the kingdom of God" (Matthew 19:24). It is similar to the purposeful exaggerations used in our time, the way someone might say, "I am so hungry I could eat all day."

Then comes Matthew 5:31-32: "It was also said, 'Whoever divorces his wife, let him give her a certificate of divorce.' But I say to you that everyone who divorces his wife, except on the grounds of unchastity, makes her an adulteress; and whoever marries a divorced woman commits adultery."

Luke 16:18 renders the same words of Jesus as, "Every one who divorces his wife and marries commits adultery, and he who marries a woman divorced from her husband commits adultery." Notice that Luke does not include an exemption for justifiable divorce, even on the grounds of unchastity or adultery. Neither does Mark (Mark 10). Luke and Mark's renditions take Jesus beyond even the strictest interpretation of the law by the Shammites. "A man who divorces his wife and marries another commits adultery." It is that final according to Luke.

The reading in Luke of what Jesus said is difficult to reconcile with the version in Matthew, in which Jesus states that porneia (unchastity) was justifiable grounds for divorce. Some scholars have concluded that Matthew added the exemption clause to the sayings of Jesus he had received. Some teach that a later scribe copyist mistakenly added the exemption to the saying. Others scoff and say that

Matthew's exemption was intentionally added by a copyist who wanted to make divorce easier.

But many hold that Matthew's are the original words of Jesus. They say that Mark and Luke did not include the exemption—either by accident, or because their readers would have taken the exemption clause to be obvious—since adultery was so radical a deterrent to continued marriage. (I recommend reading David Instone-Brewer's helpful book, Marriage and Remarriage in the Bible, for a full treatment of the subject.)

There were times when divorce was expected. It was required that a man divorce his wife if she were found to be an adulteress. In the Nativity story (Matthew 2), when Joseph decided "to divorce Mary quietly" when she was found to be expecting a child, he was acting on the Jewish law that a man could not marry his betrothed if she had violated his expectation of her virginity. Instead, Joseph kept his bride-to-be.

It would be contentious to select one report of what Jesus said and reject another. It will be far more fruitful to question why one Gospel writer told us that Jesus said it this way, another that way, and to search for harmony among the interpretations. One passage of Scripture can frequently be helpful in understanding another. The only fair judge of the words of Scripture should be other words of Scripture. It is always the sum total of what the Bible teaches that should guide us, not an isolated verse here and there. It is still true that the devil can quote scripture to evil ends. So can the opponents of evil when they decide to apply the words of Scripture to prove a conclusion previously fashioned in non-Biblical territory.

The first three Gospels have some important variations on the subject. At first glance, that awareness would seem to question the finality of the words of Jesus. But on reflection, it is aligned with the procedure Christians must follow when they approach everything Jesus said or did. There are other times in the life and teaching of Jesus when we are forced to seek harmony between Matthew, Mark, Luke, and at times, John.

For example, it is difficult to reconcile differences between the nativity stories of Luke and Matthew. It is also a mighty task to combine the resurrection narratives in all four Gospels into one unified lesson. Each writer has a distinct and unique message. What seemed important to one did not seem so to another. Although they had witnessed or read about the same incident, they recalled it differently. They do not contradict each other so much as they supplement each other.

When the Gospels were being written, each writer seems to have had a collected source of the stories of Jesus in front of them; that is, the famous "Q source," a hypothetical collection of the sayings of Jesus assumed to be circulating in the years following his death and prior to the writing of Mark, the earliest Gospel. It also seems certain that each Gospel writer had an individual source and added some unique personal recollections. We could say that while they were all reporting the same events, each had an individual spin on his message. Rather than dwell on how these changes came to be, it is far more important to know what Jesus said, and what it meant to those who first heard it. We, of course, seek to know what it should mean to us today.

We can readily assume that we do not know everything that Jesus said about marriage, divorce and remarriage. Curiously, the Gospel of John makes no reference whatsoever as to anything Jesus taught about the subject. There is no definitive statement on the topic anywhere in the Bible which we could lean on in making our decisions. That was not the purpose of the Gospels.

At the end of his Gospel, John wrote, "There are many other things which Jesus did; were every one of them to be written, I suppose that the world itself could not contain the books that would be written" (John 21:25). That is a reminder that even after we have studied and mastered all four Gospels, we are still left with a small portion of what Jesus taught and thought. It is wise to assume that John's qualifying conclusion also applies to marriage, divorce and remarriage. We have before us only a few isolated items that seemed important to the writers who, under the guidance of the Spirit, included them in the Gospels.

I choose to cover the teaching on marriage and divorce in Matthew 19:1-9 and Mark 10:1-12 together, although there are a few significant differences. In both passages, Jesus is speaking to the crowds when the Pharisees arrive to test him, which was a common occurrence. They asked him whether it was lawful for a man to divorce his wife. Matthew ends their question with "for any cause." Mark omits those words.

In Matthew, Jesus answered by referring to the verses we introduced from Genesis 1 and 2. They tell how God made male and female and intended them to be joined in marriage. Mark says Jesus launched directly into Jewish law asking, "What did Moses command you?" Matthew saves that question until later in the conversation when the topic is introduced by the Pharisees. The Pharisees respond that Moses allowed a man to terminate his marriage by issuing a certificate of divorce. Both writers agree that Jesus told the Pharisees that it was because of the peoples' hardness of heart that Moses allowed divorce, not because he wanted to.

Then comes the vital difference: In Mark's version Jesus says, "Whoever divorces his wife and marries another, commits adultery against her; and if she divorces her husband and marries another, she commits adultery." Matthew adds the most contested portion of Jesus' teaching, which we have mentioned previously: "I say to you: whoever divorces his wife, except for unchastity, and marries another, commits adultery." Luke has only a single sentence.

When Jesus told the Pharisees that Moses was forced to allow divorce because of their hardness of heart, he was referring to the time when the sinful nature of mankind began to dominate their lives. It was not that Moses wanted it that way. Jesus meant that in a perfect world, Moses would not have permitted divorce.

Next, Jesus moved the whole discussion up a step and referred to the beginning of creation. "God made them male and female. For this reason a man shall leave his father and mother and be joined to his wife, and the two shall become one flesh....what therefore God has joined together, let no man put asunder."

Later on, his disciples asked him in private what he meant, as you and I would also like to ask. We can assume they were sure he did not mean that marriage was indissoluble and could never be ended by divorce. Their experience in society and their knowledge of the Law, which permitted divorce for "indecency" and other causes, would have made such an arbitrary statement sound ridiculous.

Jesus answered the disciples' question in Mark 10:11-12, with: "Whoever divorces his wife and marries another commits adultery against her; and if she divorces her husband and marries another, she commits adultery." There the matter ends. But what does it all mean?

First, let us look at what Jesus did not mean. He did not mean that divorce was never permissible, as he seems to have said in Mark and Luke. But since the Gospel of Matthew is also the inspired word of God, we need to transfer over the Matthean exception and allow that in the case of unchastity, indecency or a shameful act, Jesus was teaching that divorce could rightfully occur. Jesus did not mean that once two people were married an unbreakable union was forged forever, no matter what transpired. His love for an abused wife would have negated that. As we are required to do elsewhere in applying the Bible's words to our modern age, we should expand the meaning of the Word beyond the four possible translations of porneia mentioned above.

The Jewish community of the 1st century A.D. agreed on other justifiable grounds for divorce in addition to sexual sins. Depriving a spouse of food and shelter, physical or emotional abuse, infertility, violence or desertion all were allowable in divorce petitions. Among the types of unfaithfulness to wedding vows were neglect, debilitating tension, failure to communicate, irresponsible and dangerous behavior and reckless use of family money.

Jesus' private discussion with the disciples raises another thorny matter. It is not clear what he meant in his reference to the woman who divorces her husband, thereby committing adultery. A Jewish woman could not divorce her husband, not in the way we view divorce in our time. She could petition him to write her a certificate of divorce, which he could refuse to do.

It appears that Jesus is speaking about a woman who deserts her husband and marries or lives with another. Some scholarly commentators note that Jesus was most likely thinking of the conduct of Herodias, who in a celebrated local scandal in Palestine, wrote an illegal letter of divorce to her husband so that she could marry King Herod Antipas, who had also dumped his wife.

In the setting of Mark, the question the Pharisees asked about divorce follows shortly after the death of John the Baptist, who had been thrown into prison and eventually beheaded, because he condemned the conduct of Herodias and Herod Antipas to the king's face (Mark 6:14f.). The concluding words of Mark 10:11-12 are more aptly explained by their relationship to the disaster that befell John the Baptist in the wake of his denunciation than they are by accepting them as a universal condemnation of a woman who divorces her husband and becomes an adulteress if she marries another. From a wife's point of view, the primary purpose for a Bill of Divorce was that it freed her to marry another.

Finally, we add an additional comment on the exception clause in Matthew; "except for unchastity." Knowing that Jesus dealt with people by the law of love, rather than with the rigidity of the Law alone, it is possible to say with confidence that the exception clause belongs to what Jesus would likely have said to those who had been deserted, defiled, abused or defeated in a marriage they had tried to save. He said in John 10:10 that he had come to bring abundant life to his people—hardly possible if one is condemned to endure an unhappy and stifling marriage doomed to failure.

The Epistles of St. Paul: Romans 7:1-4 and I Corinthians 7: 1-14

We will conclude this study of what the Bible says about divorce with a cursory look at two relevant passages in St. Paul. The ones listed above offer more than enough to understand what Paul taught about the topic. The particular interest we have in Romans 7 arises in his comments that, "A woman is bound to her husband as long as he lives." And that "she will be called an adulteress if she lives with another man as long as her husband is alive." Those sentences have often been used to prove Paul teaches that marriage is a lifelong commitment, and even if the couple is separated, the wife cannot seek other male companionship so long as her first husband is still alive. As reassuring as that teaching is to those who have decided that the Bible teaches that marriage is for life, we conclude the opposite. Paul is committed to the principle that Christian marriage should continue for "as long as both shall live."

Paul shares with his Master the high view of marriage and a lasting regret about divorce. But when you bring the other things which St. Paul wrote about marriage and divorce into view, it becomes clear that he permitted—even advised—divorce. In Romans 7:15, he writes, "But if an unbelieving partner (in the marriage) desires to separate, let it be so; in such a case the brother or sister is not bound." In other words, a believer who is married to an unbeliever is not to initiate divorce, but if the other does, the believing partner is free to divorce and marry again.

In Romans 7, Paul repeats that a woman is bound to her husband for as long as he lives. On the surface that would seem to support the argument that divorce and remarriage is denied to the woman under any circumstance. Yet in context, Paul is using marriage as a metaphor to illustrate a larger point in the surrounding text: He is actually explaining the ways in which Christ superseded the Law. In Chapters 6 and 7, he tells his readers they have died to their former lives as slaves to sin and the Law, and they are now called to a new life in Christ Jesus. They belong to him, emancipated from their former selves. To show them what he means, he refers to the above verses on marriage.

It is as if he wrote: It is like this: a woman is bound to her husband so long as he is alive and is her husband. These Christians in Rome would be bound to sin under the Law so long as the Law was in effect. But when the Law died through the redeeming death of Christ Jesus, so did the necessity to adhere to it, just as the wife is no longer bound to the law of marriage when her husband dies. Paul is not concerned here with marital sin or remarriage. The woman would become an adulteress if she took up with another man when she was still married. But if her husband were dead, or if her marriage were dead, she would be free to live a new and abundant life.

Returning to I Corinthians 7, it is important to understand that Paul was responding to questions the Corinthians had asked him in a letter. He was not writing an independent moral treatise. He tells us that in the opening words of the chapter. There is also reference to correspondence in both I and II Corinthians. It appears here that the

Corinthians had asked Paul several questions about marriage and divorce, about sexual relationships within marriage, about single men and women and widows, and how they were to handle their sexual desires.

He begins by answering that it is well for a man not to touch a woman unless tempted beyond his control. In that case he should find himself a spouse. His response does not put marriage on a pedestal so much as it becomes a vehicle to release sexual desire. Once married, the couple should not refuse each other conjugal rights, for Paul writes, "the wife does not control her own body, nor the husband his."

He also adds that "The wife should not separate herself from her husband, but if she does, let her remain single or be reconciled." The word for separate here cannot mean divorce. If she had been divorced, reconciliation would presumably be impossible, since people of the Law were not permitted to marry each other a second time. He adds (verse 15) that the believer should not divorce his or her spouse unless and until the non-believer abandons the marriage.

This all takes place within the context that he is encouraging the people of Corinth to keep things the way they are, "Whether single or married, do not wish to change it." According to Paul, the time would be exceedingly short before the Lord would return. His advice is for the time between the moment he was writing and the time that Christ would come again. The ethical/moral advice is related to the time pressure on the second coming of Christ, not on the advisability of marriage.

For us to bring this chapter to conclusion, however, we must mention The Pauline Privilege, the phrase ordinarily used in concluding that St. Paul permits divorce if the unbelieving spouse deserts the marriage. The Catholic Church permits it in dissolving marriages.

I take the Privilege much further. I have ministered to a large number of people who were deserted by their spouses. Perhaps they were not literal non-believers, as Paul would use the term. But they were not believers in Christian marriage. By that I mean that a person can pretend to be a believer in public, but is not so in private. I recall one man who was an important figure in his church. He gave generously to the poor and needy and was a leader in public philanthropic endeavors. He spread his loving kindness all over the city. One day his wife said to me, "I wish he would spread some of that kindness around here with me and our children." Sure enough, he filed for divorce not long after and ran off to marry another woman.

There are many ways that a spouse can become "a non-believer" in the marriage and offend the marriage partner. A spouse can abandon the marriage without resorting to sexual deviations or abandoning the faith. When those transgressions mount up beyond the ability to bear them, the other spouse has the privilege of responding to the critics that the marriage was deserted by "an unbeliever." I would guess that St. Paul would send back a word of approval and encourage the abandoned partner to proceed with divorce.

The brief conclusion is that the Bible is not so arbitrary on matters of marriage and divorce and remarriage as the Church often teaches. The Bible allows for a variety of causes which can bring the end of a marriage. Jesus allowed for divorce if a spouse was guilty of infidelity. I expand the word to mean not only adultery. A spouse can be unfaithful in a number of ways.

St. Paul taught that divorce is permitted if an unbeliever abandons the marriage. I expand the meaning of that word also. A man or woman can abandon the marriage in more ways than sexual misconduct with another person. He/she can be an "unbeliever" in the marriage, as of the faith. One who does not provide for a spouse, or who abuses her/him in physical or emotional ways, or who avoids meaningful marriage has deserted the marriage and the faith.

CHAPTER 3
TAKING A LAST LOOK AROUND

While this book is written for those who are divorced or divorcing, I want to say a word to those who are married and might be considering divorce: Please take a last look around. Make sure you are making the right choice, or at least the best choice available. No perfect choice is possible once you come to a moral crisis; you must choose between two imperfect options. In Moral Man in an Immoral Society, theologian Reinhold Niebuhr wrote that the Christian is always faced with that dilemma when it is time for a moral decision. We must examine the two possibilities and take the lesser of the two evils. In this case, the Niebuhrian principle would say that if it is wrong to end a marriage and break your wedding promises, it would be a poorer choice to stay and exacerbate the trouble.

To prevent making the poorer choice, walk slowly toward the line. Take a good look around. I do not mean a quick glance back over your shoulder so that you can say you fulfilled your obligation to be fair and be able to tell everyone you tried your best. I mean a long, soul-searching exercise to evaluate what happened, who was at fault, and where, when and why. A wide range of things are no doubt brewing, but usually there is a compelling reason or person which prompts the decision to separate. Divorce does not arise in a vacuum.

In graduate school we used to tease each other that insincerity is commonplace in dealing with troubled marriages. Even when both members of the marriage say they have sought an honest evaluation with objective professional help, when all the inward and outward pressures have been identified and a settlement has been forged, we still said, "You will probably meet a comely lass or handsome laddie waiting on the courthouse steps."

That might sound coarse to those who have struggled to strengthen a marriage that was doomed to failure. But I have often witnessed smokescreens of one kind or another—wild exaggerations masquerading as the truth to why the marriage failed.

Usually there is a selfish explanation: One or the other wants to move on. It need not be an issue of sex. It is not always another person. It could be a yearning to find some new purpose, to start on a new career, to capture what is left of a life that is not working, or as someone told me decades ago, the desire "to find myself." Now and then it is simply the yearning to shed the responsibilities of marriage, home and family.

Life promises more than it delivers. It looks like it should be easy to carve out a wholesome life and find happiness for the Biblical three-score-and-ten years we are given to live on the earth. But it seldom works that way. Easy Street is hard to find. Permanent peace and harmony are illusive. Selecting the compromise that works in your situation is the secret key to opening the way. The Bible knows all about human expectations and realities. "What does a man gain by all the toil under the sun? …. All is vanity and a striving after the wind" (Ecclesiastes 1). Life refuses to march to the promises of the private drums we beat.

Marriage can promise more than it delivers, too. The unrealistic expectations we heap on the institution can be so heavy that the whole relationship crumbles. One partner may bring a string of burdens to the marriage. At times they are insurmountable, expecting the magic of marriage to transform them all into blessings. Included in that list are the idiosyncrasies of the man and the woman who vow to stay together for as long as they both shall live. At times more than a secret wish or two are carried into the marriage. Imbedded in the soul and psyche of the partners is the unfinished business of prior lives, including childhood dreams and longings, encoded deep inside a search to be worthwhile. No one person can absorb all the requirements of another, especially when the list of what the other wants and needs is almost infinite.

No partner can possibly supply everything that is lacking in the other, especially when what is wanted and needed is unknown or not communicated. When that happens, it is not the marriage that fails them; they fail the marriage. In those cases, the affected partners should first seek help on their own, and then return to work on the marriage. I have often told couples that I could not work with both of them together, since the problems were personal and not marital.

When troubled couples come to visit or write to me for counsel on what to do next, I ask them to go back with me to the beginning of their relationship. I ask, "What brought you together? Why did you choose this one from all of the available mates? Why did you choose each other? What needs did you have that led you to your spouse? What did 'love' mean to you in the beginning?"

If you are thinking of divorce, I recommend that you consider the following questions: What circumstances prompted you to get married? What situation were you in or getting out of that opened the way for your willingness to marry? Most of all, what do you think made you love this person enough for you to want to spend the rest of your life together? What needs in you did he or she fulfill? Have those needs changed? How have you changed?

The answers I have heard are legion. In these changing times they have taken on a new dimension. The major change in the past few decades is the number of couples who have chosen to live together without being married. That alters the answer to why they came together. While formerly they would tell me that they decided to leave their parents' home, or they were madly in love, or they were running away from something or on the rebound from someone else, they now tend to answer that they decided to live together as a matter of convenience, or for ease of romance, or for sharing expenses, or for a trial period prior to marriage itself to see how things would work out. Many times they do not know why they came to be together. In any case, the reasons why a couple married in the first place is the first rung on the ladder to understanding what went wrong.

The second step is to discover what went wrong, and what happened to change the yearning to be a couple. I inevitably ask, "When did the trouble begin? Did some occasion initiate the reluctance to continue?" Most couples do not really know the answers, or at least one does not remember when the first sign of trouble appeared. Regardless, if love was present at the start, then something happened. The problem began at a particular time: occasionally after the birth of the first child, following the death of a parent, on the heels of a loss or change of a job, in the wake of moving away from their hometown, or when one partner began to seek recreation with friends other than the spouse.

At this point it is critical that both understand and appreciate the other's perception of how, when and why the trouble began. What one identifies might not be important at all to the other. It might not even be true. Some time ago I read Joanna's Husband and David's Wife, by Elizabeth Forsythe Hailey. David found his wife's private journal and became so involved that he wrote his own comments following each of Joanna's entries. Needless to say, they had profoundly different recollections. It is an interesting book.

But it is critical to learn why the wife or husband recalls the incident in a particular way. People often do not mean what they say, and they do not say what they mean. Since they do not normally have an intimate diary of their marriage, and they do not normally take notes on the changes that occur, the recollection is left to the happenstance of two sets of memories.

Communication—or miscommunication—is the other most common problem faced in recapitulating the events of a marriage. A misperception of what a spouse feels and believes to be true can be worse than not hearing what your partner says at all. I have watched the lights come on when one participant finally realizes what the other has been thinking, feeling or saying all along.

The third and final question I routinely ask should be obvious: "Are you both willing to try to work out the difficulties?" That sounds simple, but it takes a deep, quiet and prayerful patience to answer. Seldom are both spouses equally willing to seek help. If either one is unwilling to search through the issues to plan a course to rebuild the relationship, it is futile for the other to keep trying. It takes two to tango, and it takes two or more to put the broken pieces together again. If one is playing a game and not really trying, it is unfair and unkind to the other.

Paul writes in I Corinthians that "Love never ends." Assume that it doesn't. Why, then, do people say they have fallen out of love? There is an interlocking grid of answers. First, one has to examine whether it was "love" that brought them together in the first place. What masquerades as love in a culture fascinated with dreams of a prince or princess waiting over the next hill can be simply a convenient label for momentary attraction. If the decision to marry was based on the need to get away from somewhere or someone, or to find an independent life, or to satisfy the desires of family and friends and all the rest; then what Paul calls love was probably not present.

This brings us back to the first question: "Were you in love at the beginning, or did you step into the marriage to meet some other requirement?" If the answer is "no, we were not in love," then the question for the future is not how to rebuild the marriage, but whether the couple wants to "get married."

If the answer to the question is that it was genuine love and the desire to spend life together that brought you to the altar, then we move on to question number two: "Where, when and why did it begin to go wrong?" Of course, the couple must agree to work together on what went wrong and to try to uncover the debris that covers their love for each other.

Paul says, "Love is patient and kind." The world around us is so impatient. The world can be unkind, filled with loud noises, harsh demands, wars and worse. In a Christian home, patience and kindness should rule. My aunt used to have a sign in her kitchen that read, "Kindness Spoken Here." Not that it was always true; tension and trouble are part of living. Jesus also had moments when he was angry— surely for a righteous cause, but also out of his frustration in trying to make the world a better place.

Paul writes, "Love does not insist on its own way." My dad used to chuckle when he said, "The Bible says that the two shall become one. The problem is, which one will they be?" The willingness to talk to and listen to your spouse is required to make it through trying times.

One problem is that most men do not communicate well with their wives. Occasionally a wife never learns to talk to her husband on an equal basis. Individuals might be the best negotiators in the workplace, but they fail to acknowledge and communicate with their spouses at home. Both can "insist on their own way," until one capitulates and walks away. Each time that happens, the gulf between them grows wider. The goal of a good marriage is to have two adult people in love who are concerned for each other, not for themselves, and being able and willing to say it.

Paul also writes, "Love bears all things, believes all things, hopes all things, and endures all things" (I Corinthians 13:7). When marital pressures mount, we often fail to bear the burdens of the one we love. There are all kinds of burdens. The obvious ones include physical or emotional illness, troubles with parents or children, financial worries, and the like. But we tend to miss the inner soul and feelings of the other. The greatest pressures come from within: Our outward behavior follows inner promptings.

My first professor of counseling, Dr. Gordon E. Jackson, warned his students that they should try to lead couples away from divorce by saying, "Most couples in their second marriages sit down at the breakfast table wishing the first spouse were back." The warning might have been a trifle excessive, but it hints at an ancient truth: "The more things change, the more they stay the same." We do not drop our emotional burdens at the side of the old road when we move on. The same old person with the same old troubles travels along. I have known large numbers of married people who are unhappy, but I have also known an equal number of discontented people who are divorced. It often solves nothing at all. Therefore, I say again, take a last look around.

Love is patient. Every now and then I have remarried a couple who were divorced from each other. (I am aware that an Old Testament law was broken.) The request for the second marriage usually came at a point of crises, such as a serious illness or a tragedy involving a child. It can happen. But no one should be called on to sit around and wait for a former spouse to return. God would never require that an abandoned wife or husband remain wedded to a shattered promise forever and a disloyal partner. No one should be forced to stay married to a spouse who does not want to be married.

Now and then I see mini-miracles, where the aggrieved partner endures the situation with painstaking patience until the guilty member comes to his or her senses and initiates reconciliation. It can happen, but it is rare. It occurred with Hosea in the Old Testament. As we noted, the prophet kept waiting around for his errant wife to return. Each time she did, he welcomed her back home without hesitation or complaint, not that we know of anyway. But it is clear that his action was meant to illustrate the unwavering love God had for his people Israel. With us, waiting for someone to return is a Catch 22 kind of conundrum, with little hope of a happy ending.

If you have been honest in taking a last look around, and you have found no compelling reason to keep bashing your head against a wall, take the lesser of the two evils, or rather the better of the two, and move on.

CHAPTER 4
WHEN THE TIME FOR DIVORCE HAS COME

"There is a time for everything under the sun:
A time to be born and a time to die; a time to plant
And a time to pluck up that which is planted; …
A time to weep and a time to laugh;
A time to mourn and a time to dance,
A time to seek and a time to lose;
A time to keep and a time to cast away."

In this well-known passage from Ecclesiastes 3, the author captures the gist of our merry-go-round existence. Had he been writing today, he could have included, "There is a time to be married and a time to be divorced."

When the time for divorce has come, everyone wants to be sure. Some say it never should be. There was a time when I leaned in that direction myself. Long ago I told friends that I had counseled divorce only twice, and in both cases I was wrong. That, too, has changed.

The topic of divorce, as we have mentioned, is a long and continuing struggle among Church leaders. Even among family and friends, discussions of divorce can be as dangerous as crossing a mine field. Many Christians continue to take a hard line. Others are puzzled that a sensible writer would care to put forward what the Bible has to say. Why bother to bring the ancient word of God into a discussion of contemporary mores, they ask? Yet, many men and women are looking for guidance in this matter, which continues to be a nagging problem.

In my decades as a pastor, hundreds of people have told me that their marriages were over. Often, the request for divorce came without warning. Unfortunately, sympathy for them was often in short supply. One woman said, "When my husband left, some of my family and friends blamed me. They insinuated that if I had done this or not done that, I would have been able to keep him."

Another woman told to me that a clergyman would not marry her and her fiancé because she had been divorced. "Even though my husband ran off with our neighbor, I was told I would be living in sin if I married again. He also said I could never receive the sacrament again."

In "There is a time for everything under the sun," Ecclesiastes meant that we all live in the ebb and flow of life. Our days include a variety of experiences; some to our liking, some not. My mother used to simplify it by saying, "Some years are better than others." The author of Ecclesiastes reminds us that we also live our times by the Grace of God. We are not in charge. We pretend we have a right to a long and level path for as long as we choose. We think God will prevent us from difficulties and give us what we desire. It is not God's plan to set aside the eternal purpose of Creation to attend to our personal pleasures. There are other things to do.

We have noted in a different context that our thoughts about marriage and divorce have changed in the past half century. When I was a boy, we all assumed that marriage lasted forever. A couple promised to stay together "until death do you part," and they surely did. We now say "as long as you both shall live." Hardly anyone in our family got divorced. There were a few divorces in our neighborhood, and fewer in our little church. Although we all knew about some strange marriages, it was still understood that couples stayed together no matter what.

When a divorce occurred, someone was to blame. Either he drank too much, or she fooled around, or they both violated their promises in significant ways. With that in mind, we assumed that they got what they deserved. My father used to say that a happy husband would never look anywhere else.

I came from a "good Christian home," where it was understood the wife would devote herself to her husband, whom the Bible says is "head of the house." No matter how incapable or incompetent some husband might be, still the Head of the House made the important decisions. I used to preach the Biblical rationale that "God's order for the Christian home was that there was a top-dog husband; a willing, waiting-wife; and peace forever more, so long as she listened and obeyed.

In that naïve state, my Peggy and I were married in 1959. We did not have a philosophy of marriage. We just loved each other. As it turned out, I guess I am the head of our home, but more often I think of it as her house or our home. For years it was the children's house. She certainly ran the house while I was off working and doing the will of God. Peggy would agree that it was not always easy. Every marriage has its problems, as every life has its disappointments. But we kept on keeping on, abiding as best we could, and without bragging about it, trying with all our might to fulfill the promises we made. When I told one of our friends about this book, she said that many times she had wanted to bash her husband with a two-by-four, but she had never considered a divorce.

About three years after we were married, I received a call from a friend in Kentucky. "Richard, can you help me?" Jim pleaded. "Carolyn has left me. She said that marriage is not her thing. She is bored, not only with me, but with the whole idea of being tied down. Please talk to her. Tell her that the children and I need her. Please tell me what I did wrong, and I will change it."

I wrote back a long letter trying to explain what I thought had gone wrong. It was easy enough to blame her. The early 1960s were tumultuous years indeed. I guessed that in her disenchantment, she was looking for something new to do, some way to "find herself." I don't know if she ever found it, but troubles have a tendency to follow you around.

From what I knew, Jim believed in marriage and family. Even Carolyn admitted he was kind and caring. He tried to be a loving husband; even if no one had told him how to do it or how to manage his life with her. I concluded that the failure of their marriage did not mean that either Jim or Carolyn had failed. It just seemed that the time had come for them to be divorced.

Pondering that experience, I revised my belief that divorced people got what they deserved. Jim's frustration and Carolyn's departure validated my observation that sometimes people change. Other times, of course, someone acts out of selfish motives, or for revenge, or in a rush towards self destruction. But whatever prompts the time for divorce, the party left behind must pick up the pieces and keep on going.

Since that time it seems that someone we know files for divorce almost every time we turn around. I am often taken by surprise. As one woman told me when she asked for a divorce, "Things are not always what they seem."

In the United States, nearly half of all marriages end in divorce. In fact, 4.5 million marriages will most likely come to an end this year. Half of these couples will have been married less than five years. Twenty-five million Americans have been divorced at least once. Most divorced people remarry: three out of four women, and five out of six men. The divorce rate is almost 50 percent higher in second or third marriages. The fallout on everyone around them is tremendous.

Sometimes, the reason for divorce is a mystery. Most are the result of the complexity of our lives. We do not prepare ourselves well for marriage. Most ecclesiastical weddings include a requirement to come to the priest or pastor (or rabbi) for premarital counseling. Too often that consists of a little chat about the wedding ceremony. More emphasis on premarital marriage counseling might be helpful. Peggy and I still chuckle when we think about our "premarital counseling." The pastor took us aside and told us first that we should never complain about our in-laws to each other. Secondly, he said he thought "sex was for more than procreation." Both are good pieces of advice, even if the second reflects the tenor of the late 1950s.

Today we live in a time of immediate gratification.

People are on the lookout for instant pleasure. When they do not find it, they move on to something or someone else. The kind of commitment made in the days of yore has drifted away. Casual sexual experimentation has loosened the grip of traditional Christian morals. By the way, not complaining about your in-laws is still good advice.

We also live in a day when the role of women in the home and workplace has been rewritten. The number of demands made on wives, mothers and employees adds tremendous burdens to the marital union. Add in the demand for unbounded sexual fulfillment and satisfaction and the need to perform with excellence, and the marriage becomes more like a circus. The culture often assumes that sexual gratification is the chief end of marriage.

As women's possibilities were broadened, their ability to find a life outside the home was enhanced as well. Increasing options for everyone puts pressure on all of us, especially on growing children. But whatever the impediments are which interfere with a successful marriage, if nothing can be done to remove them; the time for divorce has come.

It is sad to say that divorce marks the death of a marriage, but it is true. Unlike the death of the physical body, which comes as a welcomed relief if pain and suffering have been intolerable and viable life has vanished, the death of a marriage seldom brings extended feelings of relief. No sophisticated explanation can dissuade us from this obvious truth. While the marriage bond should not be easily broken, once it is broken, the marriage is dead, and the time has come to give it a proper burial.

That moment comes with great sadness. No one ever

looks back over the lifetime of a marriage without some regret and guilt. There is always more that we could have done. But there is no use living in the past. God does not permit us to go backwards. He is always moving us toward the future. Try not to hold on to a marriage when it is over and done, or you might bury yourself alongside your marriage. Take custody of you.

I mentioned that in my early years, I used to preach that divorce was wrong. I pontificated that a woman should take care of her husband, home and children, and the husband should take care of the rest. I declared that each of us had God-given duties. To shirk them is anathema to God and man. It sounded great to some husbands, whose ears perked up when they heard me preach a family sermon.

One Sunday after services, I met a young woman at the back door of the church with tears in her eyes. "Dr. Cromie," she said sadly, "I tried everything you said for 12 long years. I devoted myself completely to my husband, to our children and to the needs of both. I got little in return for me, but I kept on doing it as a good Christian wife. Two months ago, my husband told me he did not love me anymore and ran off to marry his secretary. Our 'model marriage' was over. He's gone. What am I supposed to do now?"

She had been totally faithful to her wedding vows and her responsibilities to her husband and family, but he chose to desert it all for another woman. "What am I supposed to do now?" is an elementary question, terse and to the point. My answer, unfortunately, was delayed until now. But I say clearly that you should not try to stay married to a partner who does not want to be married to you. You cannot. It is not a matter of damage to your pride or hubris; it is a simple fact. How could you ever do it? Unless you choose to be a grass widow or to wait around for your partner to return, the time for divorce has come.

CHAPTER 5
FIRE IN THE STABLES

When I was growing up in Pittsburgh, Pennsylvania, my father used to take me to Schenley Park to visit the Carnegie Museum, the Art Galleries, the Cathedral of Learning and the Phipps Conservatory. The park had beautiful ponds and gardens that overlooked the public golf course. I visited often during the 47 years I lived in Pittsburgh.

At the top of the park there used to be a riding stable, where for a few cents you could take a pony ride around the oval. As we grew older, we progressed from pony treks to unescorted horseback rides along the trail through the woods, pretending to be famous cowboys hustling down the path. I still recall that when we turned around to head back to the stable, the horses would begin to gallop. They were in a hurry to get home, where they knew they were safe.

This leads me to the story of that awful day when the unimaginable took place: The stables caught on fire and burned to the ground. The horses trapped inside perished in the flames.

But something more bizarre also happened. When the fire broke out, some of the horses were grazing in the paddock across the road. As the sirens blared, and the fire trucks clanged up from Station Number Four, and the grooms were rushing about, screaming for help to save the horses trapped inside, those who were safely out in the field became terrified and panicked. Believing that the safest place for them was back inside the stable, their home, a few of them broke loose from their tethers, jumped or broke the fence, and rushed across the street into the stables, where they perished along with the others.

I have never forgotten it, and it stands as a symbol of my approach to divorce. The memory warned me never to rush back to the days of yore. It has helped me continue moving forward. It has also assisted me in counseling others to beware of turning back toward a home, job, lifestyle, relationship or marriage that was not safe.

Robert Fulguhm, the sometime minister and author of a delightful book called, All I Really Need to Know I Learned in Kindergarten, wrote another book called, It Was on Fire When I Lay Down on it. This book tells the story of a small-town Emergency Squad that was summoned to a burning house where a person was trapped inside. They broke in and found a man half asleep on a smoldering bed. After hosing the mattress and rescuing him, they asked how the mattress caught on fire. "I don't know," he muttered. "It was on fire when I lay down on it."

The story is funny, of course, but Fulguhm turns it into a symbolic reminder for everyone. We can be guilty of making our own troubles, or at least of contributing to them, by returning to times and places that were not good for us then or now. St. Paul laments in Romans, "I cannot understand my own actions. For I do not do the thing I want, but I do the very thing I hate…" (Romans 7:15). It's like the old chestnut, "We make our own beds, and then we lie in them."

My purpose in including the story of the fire in the stables is to caution those whose time of divorce has come, not to rush back into a burning marriage for sake of tradition, promises, family urgings or feelings of safety. Unless something major has changed that caused the fire to go out, it would be futile and self destructive to go back in. The future is now. It begins this very moment. Seize it and go forward.

CHAPTER 6
THE AFTERSHOCKS OF DIVORCE

We tend to feel safe on this big, old, sturdy planet where we walk confidently about, as if it were secure and will last forever. The problem is that it isn't and it won't. The Atlantic seaboard and Gulf Coast states know all about the horrors of hurricanes. Tornados threaten almost everywhere. Volcanoes, fires and floods still wreak their havoc, not to mention the massive tsunami that killed more than a quarter million people in Southeast Asia the day after Christmas 2004.

Although aftershocks of one kind or another can follow any of the above, the word is normally reserved for earthquakes. In a California quake in 1994, a huge fissure brought down buildings and bridges and roadways. It also brought down the confidence of those who had experienced it. The disruption of the earth and of human life did not end with the quake, since 4,000 smaller earthquakes were recorded in the days and months that followed. They did not rival the first in power or duration, but they did cause damage and upset the equilibrium of those who had to endure them. Geologists say that aftershocks are necessary. The broken land has to resettle into its new configuration above and below the surface. But aftershocks can be unnerving.

In addition, there are phenomena known as "phantom earthquakes." They cause a person to feel as if the earth were shaking when it is not. Psychologists say the apparitions intrude on daily life for weeks, months or years after an earthquake, as the intensity of the initial experience works its way to the surface of the brain.

Those who have been through divorce are well aware of aftershocks. A feeling of relief generally comes when the divorce decree is finally granted. But the maelstrom of feelings that follow can be devastating. One woman told me that her worst moment came on her way home from the courthouse. "Up to the last moment, I kept thinking he would call the lawyer and cancel the whole thing, but he didn't. I never realized that I was actually going to be severed permanently from the wonderful life we enjoyed for 30 years. I was fooling myself that it would be an ordinary day," she told me.

Another said, "Thank God they require a personal witness to testify at your hearing. It never occurred to me that I would have such a demoralizing reaction. If Janie had not been there, I think I would have jumped off the nearest bridge. I was not prepared for the emotional, soul-destroying jolt the divorce decree gave me. I was shaking." Yet she had known the divorce was coming for more than a year.

Routine adjustments that have to be made are difficult enough, but at least they are more or less predictable. Certain tried and tested procedures can lead you through them. Self-help divorce manuals catalogue the range of difficulties to expect: finding new friends, dating, handling household chores, eating meals alone, dealing with former in-laws, making financial readjustments, arguing for custody, holidays, clubs and churches, guiding children, and more. They are legitimate concerns and difficult ones. Handling them successfully is critical to making a readjustment.

But there are deeper and more subtle aftershocks, which are harder to describe and impossible to predict. They have to do with inner fears and uncertainties, some of long standing. They roam the corridors of the memory of all that might have been. They wander around in the cellar of self confidence, popping up now and again with insidious challenges and outrageous questions like, "Was it really all his fault?," or, "Am I a loser?"

These aftershocks spawn awkward hypothetical situations, such as "If I had only done this, she might not have done that, and we would still be together." Or, "What if I am like my mother as he always said I was?" Or, "Was she right in saying that I don't know how to talk to women?" "Was I an accomplice in his drinking, an enabler who should have sought help?" "I wonder if I am afraid of my own body, as he used to say when I was not a cooperating partner in sex." "Was I too bossy and controlling?" These kinds of questions wait for you when you sit down at the end of a day. They contain at minimum a touch of truth, or they would not linger as unwanted intruders.

Shattered feelings and aftershocks hold more sway over you than anyone else could ever know. They make you want to run and hide. They can derail your recovery time. Just when you thought you were getting over it, you see someone who looks like him, or talks like her or you hear a special song on the radio, or you meet a friend you haven't seen for years and for no apparent reason, the earth shakes again. An aftershock takes you by surprise. Often, it comes and goes in an instant. Sometimes it rumbles on for days.

"I start to cry at the oddest times when there is nothing to cry about," one woman told me. A "phantom shock" sets in and chases you down the road. People who try to be helpful can trigger them as well. They say things that can disturb you and reduce you to rubble, and they don't even know it. Old letters turn up in the attic search for what to throw away. Old hurts slide below the surface of the daily merry-go-round. And there are long days and nights to fill again. One woman told me she couldn't throw out all the photographs he was in because the children were usually in them, too. So she made two separate boxes of photo albums and hid one away.

At a deeper level, little whispers of self-doubt and questions of self-worth come creeping in. "Whatever did I do to deserve this?" "Why is it happening to me?" "I know God does not punish us this way, but it seems like he is." "Is there something I did not do, or something I did and never knew it?" Parents, family and friends can be a ready source of help, but often their very presence reminds you of their disappointment and secret recrimination.

Some of these questions will be hard to bear for those who have gone or are going through separation. This book is supposed to help. I include this section to be realistic and to identify the insecure child who lives within us all. I open these feelings of doubt and bravado in hopes that they will not hinder you from taking full custody of you. One friend said that as she looked back she realized she had never really shown up for her marriage – meaning, her body and voice and presence were there. She heard herself say "I do," but the total person made in the image of God had been hidden away for years.

The breaking up of a home and the lives of those who used to live there is a sad and wrenching time. Unless you decide to do something to rearrange your future, it can turn into a complete waste. If you take hold of it and move it forward to a new life, you can overcome the hurt and become a better person.

I counsel those who refuse to take advantage of the transitions in their lives that they need to initiate, not just react. God can make you a better person, but you need to help. Be still and give the Lord time to do it. I see frightened people jump from one job to the next, one relationship to another, one thrill to the next, one church to another, always looking, wishing, and hoping this new one will be the right one. But, in the rush, they do not notice that their nemeses travel along with them. They keep chasing down the road after you. You can't run away from you. Stop, look and listen to yourself!

Some people rush from one marriage to another. Sometimes they do it to prove they are desirable and capable of finding another spouse. Sometimes the next mate is sought to overcome the ennui of being alone. Sometimes the new marriage is for vengeance, to get even by showing the one who left that you are still desirable. It can take place simply to have someone to lavish love on. One divorcée asked, "What am I supposed to do with all this love when there is no one to give it too?"

You can't run away from yourself. You can move to a new town, a new job, or hurry half way around the world. But the same old person, with the same old problems, and the same old insecurities and fears follows along. Unless and until you know what motivates you from the inside, you can never jettison the problems of the past.

Nothing less than a self-examination of the soul and psyche is required. If you have never done it before, now is the time. If you refuse this time of meditation, you could ruin your chance at a wholesome relationship in the future.

When the transition is finally over, you want to stand tall, and be proud of who you see in the mirror. As you face divorce, friends can surely help you. Professional guidance will probably be beneficial. Men may be reluctant to seek help with their inner struggles. But as we all try to have an annual physical examination, it is also wise to have an annual spiritual and emotional examination. A strong faith can also help. The greatest help, the best way you can begin to help YOU is to look within own soul and psyche.

> *This above all:*
> *To thine own self be true*
> *And it must follow,*
> *As the night the day,*
> *Thou canst not then*
> *Be false to any man.*
> WILLIAM SHAKESPEARE, FROM HAMLET

There is no shame in discovering who you are inside, and less shame in saying that you need help to uncover it. If you find that you also were responsible for the breakdown of your marriage, that is acceptable too. Human beings were not intended to be perfect. That is what the Garden of Eden story of creation is all about. God is perfect; you do not have to be. The Creator allows you to be human. If you deny and avoid the humanity of weakness, it will crop up and knock you down with a certain phantom quake.

An older friend of mine died suddenly in his 40s more than 40 years ago. I was mystified by his sudden departure. He had been a good friend to me as I was growing up. He was the first person I was close to who passed away. I asked a member of his family what happened, why he had died. The minister said in the service that, "It was God's will, or Bill would still be here." I couldn't bear the thought of that, even then. But one of Bill's closest friends told me that while he did not know why people died of heart attacks, he did know that "Bill had always seemed to be running away from himself, always in hiding, always looking for an escape."

If one marriage partner or the other goes through that masquerade and tries to escape, or are hiding from others and themselves, if they are looking for an escape it is little wonder that things do not work out. All their relationships are threatened. The marriage will be doomed, and nothing will be learned from the divorce.

If you are fragile and incapable of listening to honest criticism, even from yourself, you should begin to re-focus your introspection. If you can identify the path you took to get where you are, at least you have a chance of following your footsteps back to where you were when you had hold of things.

If you know the origin of your fears, then even if you cannot overcome them, at least you can make friends with them and identify where they hide. If you know where your fears and foibles are hiding, you should be able to avoid them, or if they turn up, to fend them off. They will not be able to sneak up on you and level you with another aftershock. Hopefully, a happy new marriage will last you all your days.

———————•———————

We need to accentuate the positive as well. We should not forget the good lessons that linger long after the shock of divorce and separation is over. Most of us who have been through hurricanes, earthquakes and personal tragedies carry with us warm and wonderful memories about how people survived by taking care of other people, and by focusing on themselves and their capabilities.

There is a hero in your soul, an indelible tangible yearning to get beyond the trying moments and to help others to get beyond theirs, as well. St. Paul calls it "your higher self." Your lower self is also there. Often, they war with each other. But the higher side will take command as soon as you release it to. You must believe in you. In overcoming divorce or grief or illness or loneliness or fear, it is astonishing how absolutely heroic ordinary human beings can become, even with minimum adjustment.

How others have found courage in divorce can be a marvelous aid. In the middle of adversity, people gain or are given a new confidence. Some become even smug about how they managed to survive the worst. One British friend of mine still loves to tell the story of how he managed to survive in the tubes of the subway system under the streets of London when Hitler's bombs rained down during World War II. Under pressure, we are all capable of extraordinary achievements. When you bounce back, you feel proud and confident. It is also true following divorce.

Albert Schweitzer once wrote about "the fellowship of those who bear the mark of pain." They know each other on sight, just by looking. They recognize each other without asking or answering. They live in the knowledge that the adverse forces of human existence have done their worst and still have not conquered. If you can stare into the abyss and come back smiling, you are on your way to glory.

Schweitzer said it in a lofty and meditative way. But I also like the way the actor Broderick Crawford put it: "Once in a while you have to do something which scares the hell out of you, or you turn into jelly."

In the Book of Hebrews we read, "Lift up your drooping hand and strengthen your weak knees and make a straight path for your feet so that you may not be put out of joint but be healed" (Hebrews 12:12). That is to say, what we take to be the bad things in life happen for a purpose. Or more exactly, when they happen we can turn them into our purpose for a good, happy, holy future. God promises it, but you and I must deliver it.

God can, and does, work all things together for good if you live in his time and are attached to his purpose. We all love the sunshiny days along the shore. A good and happy marriage is one of the finest blessings life can give. Golfer Gary Player said that, "If you have a good wife, you have a good life." To be loved by someone you love is near enough our primary purpose here upon the earth.

We all embrace the glory of this life, especially when it is going our way. But we learn more about ourselves in the darkness of the night. Nobody covets an earthquake or the aftershocks which follow; nobody wishes for a bad marriage and divorce. But if you are prepared to bring all the skills you have to endure it, you will be stronger for it and a more capable child of God.

A healthy reappraisal of yourself, by yourself at the time of your transition from divorce into whatever lifestyle you choose will not only do you a world of good, but it will also be a God-send to those around you.

A young man I met from California who had been a victim of the aftershocks of a recent earthquake told me how he finally got over it. At a family gathering in New Hampshire where he was helping cook on an outdoor grill, he suddenly felt a phantom aftershock trembling beneath him. "Impossible", he murmured, "I am as far away from California as I can get and still be in America." Then he stomped the ground with all his might and shouted, "Enough!" The aftershocks heard him I guess, for they went away for good. He was ready for the next step in his life.

Chapter 7
Let Guilt and Anger Go

Each of us has a reservoir of hidden emotions that trigger our behavior. At times they can benefit and protect us; at other times they are self-defeating. In order to use them to advantage or to neutralize them, it is mandatory that we recognize them and identify the situations that catapult them to the surface. It may be Psychology 101, but in my four decades of dealing with marriage and divorce, I have seen only a few who have put it into practice.

For example, I have a friend who does not like to be alone. If his wife leaves him by himself, even for a short time, and he does not know where she is, he gets frantic, then furious. He told me it is not because he is jealous. I asked him why it upset him, and he said he did not know. But it happens over and over again.

I knew another man who was compulsive about being on time. It was an unforgivable sin to be late for a meeting with him. If his wife did not arrive the moment he expected her, he became angry and usually started a battle. When I asked him why he felt so strongly about time, he said he really didn't know. "Maybe I inherited it from my mother," he suggested.

I knew a woman who could not communicate with her

husband on important issues. Sometimes she remained silent; other times she flew off the handle. Negotiation was not possible. She said she did not know why she acted that way. Later, she admitted that Tom reminded her of her father. "Disagreements were never allowed in our home. It was either Dad's way or no way," she said. "Now, I can't disagree with anyone without getting nervous and defensive. Afterwards, I feel guilty because I tried to stand up for myself."

You might have guessed that all three of these marriages ran into serious trouble. In two, an amicable divorce was out of the question. When people do not know why they do or say the things they do, good relationships are difficult. In the intimacy of marriage, they are impossible.

To gain custody of you, you will have to overcome these emotional pitfalls. Let me narrow it here down to two: guilt and anger, and how those emotions can cause grief. There are others which are important, like self-pity and depression and insecurity, but these two stand out among the most powerful forces in our personalities, and they abound in most divorces. When we become aware of reactions that retard our maturity, the topics of guilt and anger come to the fore. These two are so intertwined with inner needs and past voices that they will deter your search for peace within.

In order to control anger and guilt, you must determine what causes them in the first place. If you are susceptible to outbursts of anger, or if you fall to pieces when guilt or self-pity surfaces, you need to have a little talk to yourself. You need to ask who or what is in charge of you, and where your feelings come from. Maybe you never had custody of you. We are all under the tutelage of our parents and others during childhood years. It does not take Sigmund Freud to tell us that what we learn and absorb in that time shapes the persons we become.

At about the time I was ordained, W. Hugh Misseldine published a wonderful book titled, Your Inner Child of the Past. Like others in the earlier years of psychology, he attempted to unmask the "strangers" who march up and down the corridors of our personalities. He felt that an inner child from the past influences us throughout our lives, cropping up at the most awkward times and places. Freud said the same thing from a different point of view.

Misseldine said these inner children act like they are on their own. For example they help evaluate for you what another person means, like husbands who assume they know what their wives are thinking. They wander back and forth in your marital communication. He also quipped that four people go on the honeymoon: the bride, the groom and the inner child of each, adding that it makes for an overly crowded marital bed.

Discovering how and why we become the people we are is a complex and individual journey, but well worth the trouble to begin. If you don't, you will become a perennial victim of that little person within your psyche.

I offer one suggestion: Since you bring your inner-child with you wherever you go, it would be good to get to know it, so you can marshal its energies in the right direction. Whether you are married, single or in transition, your search for a new life will be held hostage by its presence unless and until you take control.

Even if personalizing the inner child seems extreme, it is certain that the influence of your past does not end when you leave your childhood home. I have met some married people who are still under the control of manipulative parents who cannot or will not let go. Some people surrender their custody to a demanding husband or wife or to the needs of their children. In other words, they never were and are not in charge of themselves. For most people, taking full custody requires a battle.

About anger

Webster defines anger as "a strong feeling of displeasure or rage." One researcher on marriage and divorce estimated that more than 75 percent of separating spouses are cauldrons of anger. The power of anger is as far-reaching as any emotional power on earth. It destroys homes and marriages. It distorts the lives and futures of children. It passes its venom from one next generation to the next. It is often uncontrollable in the sense that there is no way to ward it off. It dips its menacing tentacles into communities, Christian homes and churches, upsetting everyone and everything in its path. At its worst, it leads to physical and verbal abuse, even to injury and death.

The sources of anger are legion and impossible to dissect completely. One speculation is that our ancestors required anger for survival. This does not mean that the most ferocious necessarily won the battle for food and mates and territories. But students of the subject agree that something like anger was necessary to enable hunters to go after their prey and kill both the prey and the people who stood in their way. Gentler forces were also necessary for survival, but those who were best prepared to defend themselves and their offspring were usually the ones who made it to the next generation.

A second source of anger arises as we grow. Here too, there are situations where anger is helpful. We could say that a hungry child who screams for food is exerting a kind of natural anger against the fear of starvation. A child who feels rejected and unloved when left alone may develop problems with self-esteem that transfer to anger. Early jealousy in family or social settings can also cause resentment and anger.

It is basic psychology to say that the anger an individual feels is passed on to others. If it doesn't, it dives inside the psyche. If someone I love and trust betrays me, my anger comes in part from the betrayal, but it also comes from sources that have little to do with the incident. If expression of that anger is withheld, it erupts somewhere else.

In a nutshell: Each of us has a native predisposition as well as a learned response to anger in our make-up. Add situational anger—that is, anger arising in a particular situation, even righteous indignation against the unfairness of the world around us—and the pattern continues. Feelings of failure and disappointment release hidden anger, which can make an impact in unpredictable and disastrous ways.

Conquering anger

The conquest of anger begins with awareness that these secondary situations exist, and that our response to them is part of our coping mechanisms. One psychologist warned that you have to get your anger before it gets you. We learn to subjugate its power by recognizing the times and situations that prompt the response, and then diffuse them before they begin.

Anger itself is not wrong. No one should feel guilty about being angered by the betrayal and rejection of a spouse. Many times the offending spouse is skilled at making their marriage partner feel guilty. I heard one pastor say with a chuckle, "I am so good at apologizing, that she thinks it was her fault in the first place." It is permissible to declare that you are angry—even in a harsh, loud voice—so long as your anger is in keeping with the offense. Anger is imbedded in our makeup for the purpose of protecting us and what we believe, and for getting what we need to survive.

Professional help may be needed to modify your anger if it gets out of control. If that is not possible, a personal tour of the feelings and situations that unleash anger is essential. Try to identify the last time your anger was out of control. Then ask yourself what pushed you over the edge. Finally, think of ways you might identify and control your anger in the future. Otherwise, you will remain a prisoner of your past, and the same pattern will follow you as you seek to improve your marriage or to recover from a divorce.

St. Paul warns, "Be angry, but do not sin; do not let the sun go down on your wrath" (Ephesians 4:26). The Bible frequently speaks of "the wrath of God" and of the proper place anger has in creation. But we need to learn to let it go. In the Sermon on the Mount, Jesus advised that we should "let the day's own trouble be sufficient for the day" (Matthew 6:34). It is a good idea to review each day as it comes to an end, and let anger rest until tomorrow. In her biography, actress Mercedes McCambridge explained that after her long struggles with drugs and alcohol were over, she would congratulate herself each evening that she had made it through another day.

If anger is a compelling issue in your life, resolve each day to conquer and contain it. Congratulate yourself each time you do. Your goal is not to eliminate anger, but to control it so that it does not control you. Before you re-enter an old relationship or enter a new one, make sure that unhealthy anger is not dogging your steps.

When Peggy and I got married, my father-in-law, Melvin, took us aside and nervously told us to be good to each other. Then he shared that he and Catherine took a little time before they went to sleep each night to make sure that all was well. If anger or disappointment had been present during the day, apologies were made with a promise not to carry the troubles over to a new day. This assurance was sealed with a kiss. I am sure there were times when anger did not recede and disappear in that routine gesture. However, their routine is a good reminder that we need to address the issue of anger repeatedly with ourselves and the ones we love. And it does not hurt to anticipate a little kiss each and every night.

I end with the Serenity Prayer: "God, grant me the serenity to accept the things I cannot change; the courage to change the things I can; and the wisdom to know the difference."

About guilt

Webster defines guilt as, "the state of one who has committed an offense," and guilty as, "feelings of culpability for imagined offenses or inadequacies." Both are applicable to marriage and divorce. There is an enormous difference between what I call "being guilty" and "feeling guilty." The first is usually justified. We can, do and should feel guilty when we have done something that has hurt someone we love. Feeling guilty about something we have not done, however, should be brought to the surface, dealt with and thrown out.

Long ago one of my psychology professors carried a 12-pound sack of potatoes into the classroom. He asked for volunteers to come forward, and told them to hoist it up onto a shoulder and to hold it there for a minute or two. I was young and fit. I lifted it easily. But I soon began to feel its weight. He likened the heavy sack to the emotional weight that guilt places on the psyche. It is heavy, very heavy. If you do not release it, it will weigh you down and wear you out.

In the 12-step recovery process embraced by Alcoholics Anonymous, the fourth step is "to make a searching and fearless; moral inventory of ourselves." The fifth step is "to admit to God, to ourselves and to another human being the exact nature of our failures." Those are difficult steps to take, I am told. They require soul-searing, total honesty. But those steps can be helpful in managing the burden of guilt that follows divorce.

It does not matter whether you were the passive one or the aggressor in a break-up, guilt follows both. It does not matter which one of you violated your marriage vows, the marriage is wrecked. A critical step is to enumerate the things you did that contributed to the split. That takes an honest moral inventory of all the things that transpired since the beginning of the marriage, and sometimes even before that. It must be a fearless inventory.

Some bring guilt with them into a marriage. I recall one woman who told me her husband made her feel guilty. He responded that she felt guilty all her life about everything, and he had known her since high school. People who spend an inordinate portion of their emotional energy feeling guilty may have been guilty of some offense, but surely, not one that would create perpetual guilt. This makes it impossible to identify situations in which you are truly guilty and in need of correction.

Guilt is a normal part of life. Its origins are difficult to trace. It probably helped our forbearers blend into groups rather than continue striving for individual supremacy. As communities began to form, and concern for the group trumped that of the individual, the motivation provided by guilt became necessary to ensure a protective social unit.

It borders on oversimplification to say that early childhood training is a source of guilt. I mention briefly the inordinate influence of early religious training in perpetuating feelings of guilt. Church leaders must be especially careful in what they teach children. Feelings of guilt before the Lord are drummed into children before the time they can evaluate the situation. Pressure to conform to certain behavior or risk the withdrawal of love can seep inside. Abraham Maslow, one of the originators of behaviorist psychology, wrote that he never met anyone under age 50 who had reached maturity, and almost no one at any age who was free from feelings of guilt.

The voices of the inner child can have a lasting impact. They make you the enemy of you. That is not a good situation. It is impossible to please a perfectionist parent. Unrealistic expectations of certain families or nationalities can result in continual disappointment. Feelings of unworthiness can turn into guilt.

Removing guilt

We all feel guilty when we fail to do something we should, or when we do not measure up to expectations. In this respect, guilt has a proper place. It can be a motivating factor in moving us forward. But when it is excessive and self destructive, it is time to move it away.

In order to let go of guilt and take custody of you, some drastic personal action may be required. If you decide to escape from that little jerk of a memory lurking inside your heart and soul, then you need to initiate a fearless moral inventory of you and your marriage. You need to evaluate the reasons for your divorce. Most of all, you must take an inventory of yourself and everything you long to be with the purpose of finding your way back to what you were and forward to where you want to be.

Let guilt and anger go. Otherwise, you will punish the ones you love. Moreover, you will punish yourself.

Chapter 8
Forgiveness Is More Than Golden

Unless and until you have forgiven the one who wronged you in your marriage, until you have accepted the forgiveness of God, and unless you have learned to forgive yourself, you will carry an unnecessary burden. When you offer and receive forgiveness, you will be able to drop your burden by the side of the road and move forward to the new life waiting for you.

There is important Biblical background in this matter of forgiveness, which lies near the heart of the Christian Gospel. It is the means God uses to bring his errant children back into the fold. Original sin drove Adam and Eve out of the Eden. But the Lord did not desert them, although the Creator was disappointed when they disobeyed His command.

Throughout the Old Testament, God tried a variety of remedies to redeem the people. The patriarchs, priests, prophets and kings tried to assuage the Lord's anger; each had a turn, as did sacrifice and worship. But nothing worked.

The Lord even provided a scapegoat to carry their sins away. Leviticus 16:21f describes the origin of the Day of Atonement, a Jewish holiday. Aaron, the brother of Moses and the chief priest of the people, was ordered to bring two goats into the temple: one for the Lord, the other "for Azazel." Azazel can refer to the goat itself or to the wilderness destination where it would be sent.

The first goat, the one given to the Lord, was sacrificed on the altar. Aaron then placed his hands on the head of the second goat and "confessed over him all the iniquities and transgressions of the people Israel." With the sins of the people heaped on its back, the second goat was led into the wilderness.

The goat was "bearing all their iniquities," taking away their sins. Our familiar word "scapegoat" originates with that episode from Leviticus. A scapegoat in our culture is one who is blamed, or who chooses to accept the blame, for another.

So great and repetitious were the people's sins that the ceremony of the two goats had to be repeated every year. Slaughtering goats and lambs on the altar seems so grotesque that we can barely imagine it in a worship setting. To the Old Testament Israelites, however, it was necessary payment for the sins of mankind. Christians subsequently believed that the ultimate sacrifice of the Lamb of God on the Cross of Calvary carried away the sins of God's people forever. This eliminated the need for a yearly repetition of the ceremony.

However, the need to complete the cycle of forgiveness has not disappeared. As of old, individuals must first admit and confess their shortcomings before the Lord. Then the redeeming sacrifice of Jesus Christ is offered. But it must be accepted before the cycle is complete. As we say repeatedly in our recitation of the Lord's Prayer, "Forgive us our sins, as we forgive those who have sinned against us." They go together. You can't have one without the other.

When it comes to this book, the moral is simple: Unless and until we receive forgiveness and offer forgiveness to another as well as to ourselves, our sins, guilt and anger still have custody of us.

When you forgive a person who has wronged you, you release your burden of carrying it around. You send it away on the back of forgiving love, just as the scapegoat carried the transgressions of the ancient Israelites out into the wilderness.

If you refuse to do so, if you hold on to your grudge, or if you fail to analyze and correct yourself, you will never return to normalcy. You can release yourself, or more accurately you will be released, if you accept and share the power of forgiveness, which is more than golden. We believe that Jesus died that we might be forgiven, but we cannot fully embrace this concept until we accept it for ourselves and pass it on to the others in our world. Without it, we will wander around the edges, when we could be enjoying the treasures of the abundant life. Some people spend their emotional energies burying their hurt and resentment or trying to get even. You should allow the Lord God to handle it for you and to carry it away. Anger can poison us and who we long to be. We still need to forgive the ones we have wronged; "We love as He first loved us."

I have seen this happen with people who were abused, neglected or denied a fair share of what they expected to receive. I have seen it in the resentment of those who feel they were shortchanged in the physical, mental or emotional capabilities they received at birth, or which occurred through illness or accident. I have seen it stifle those who have lost someone they loved too much to lose. I have watched the self-inflicted pain in those who continue to pursue goals they will never achieve. The failure to forgive is the leading retardant to achieving self-esteem, which is a prerequisite for all who decide to take custody of themselves.

Paul said it best when he referred to the one thing he had decided to do: "Forgetting what lies behind and straining forward to what lies ahead, I press on toward the goal for the prize of the upward call of God in Jesus Christ. Let those of us who are mature be thus minded" (Philippians 3: 13-15). Those verses are powerful, indeed. While we often hear about the goal and the forgetting, we seldom absorb the part about its role in being mature.

If you allow guilt and anger to creep into the driver's seat of your life, you will never get where you want to go. Your steering wheel will be in the hands of someone or something else. Your constant wrestling for control will defeat yourself and others in your world. If you hold on to remorse, you will dwell in the past rather than in the future.

Sure, there may have been things you should never have done. Sure, you hurt those you said you loved, or at least you did not give them all you could have. Sure, you are not a perfect person. But the point is that since Jesus Christ is perfect, you do not have to be. God loves you as you are.

Our own self-esteem is threatened by what we think others think of us, and by what we believe God thinks about us. If there is a single underlying problem I see as a common denominator among almost all personal problems I encounter in others, it is lack of self-esteem—a failure to embrace life as a special gift from God.

If you have fallen victim to that shortfall of humanity in

your marriage or divorce, I recommend you sit down with yourself and begin to work it out. If it gets too complex or complicated, I encourage you to seek pastoral or professional counseling. There is no shame in being lost in the confusion of transition. These are uncharted waters, but guides can help show you the way.

I often use an analogy in my own counseling. If you break a leg or tear some muscles, and as a result are unable to walk on your own, you would go to a doctor for help. As you recover, you are allowed to hobble on a cane or crutches to help you along. No one will ridicule you or consider you weak.

Likewise, when emotional and mental pressures cause a tear in your equilibrium, and you find it difficult to make it on your own, there is no shame in asking for help. The monumental transition of divorce can rip your emotional stability and break the bones of your normally competent self.

I compare a visit to a counselor or psychiatrist, the medications they might prescribe, and their assistance in working through the morass of conflicting feelings as a kind of emotional crutch—no less important, no less helpful, and with no cause for shame or regret.

The power of forgiveness for you and for others in your world is a rich, rare resource, too often overlooked. Professor Donald Baillie used to say from his lofty theological chair at St. Mary's College, "Our casual attitude toward sin and its forgiveness belies a profound ignorance of human nature and our needs." The most common Greek word for forgiveness in the New Testament actually means "to set loose," or release, as to release a captive from prison or to cancel a large debt. That is the meaning we intend here. When you accept forgiveness or offer it to another and forgive yourself, it is as if you are released from prison or relieved of a huge debt you could not pay. What a happy day!

Think for a moment about someone who has wronged you, and you have allowed the insult to carry on and on. Every time you see this person, or the name comes up in conversation, the wound is reopened. You find yourself avoiding places and occasions where the person might turn up. Your last thought at night is what they did to you. You feel cheated over and over.

But if you forgive that person, you free yourself from the hold this person has over you. It is ridiculous to allow another's misdeed to predetermine what you will or will not do. If the person was rotten, let him or her live with that sack of potatoes, not you. Life is tough enough already. If you chase the sin into the wilderness and allow God to take it away, you can dance down the street with a sprightly step.

Sometimes the hardest job of all is forgiving yourself. You are allowed to make mistakes. You are allowed to fail. One failure does not a failure make. You have permission to get angry, so long as the anger does not dominate your days and years. Christ gives you permission to be human.

We appear as perfect in the eyes of God when Jesus Christ dwells in us. God does not see us as ourselves, but as reflections of His son, who dwells inside. He will dwell in you, just as he promised. He will come into your heart, hopes, goals and dreams. All you have to do is ask.

But He will not enter if you try to reserve a corner for the resentment you feel towards another, or save a spot where the past continues to reign. You must surrender everything. If not, Christ will simply hold back and wait until you clear out the trash so that his purity and love can enter in. Revelation 3:20 sums it up nicely: "Behold, I stand at the door and knock; if anyone hears my voice and opens the door, I will come into him and eat with him, and he with me." He stands outside your door and knocks, but He will not enter without an invitation. There is no room for both Christ and you to be in charge. You do not want or need two captains on your ship as you pass over troubled waters. So believe in the good news of the Gospel: in Jesus Christ we are forgiven, for now and ever more.

CHAPTER 9
WATCH OUT FOR THE CHILDREN

Our purpose in this book is to focus on the need to take custody of you as you go through conflict, separation and divorce. As a child of God, it is your sacred right and duty. However, you may have to take custody of your children, as well. Including this forceful little chapter does not diminish the prior obligation. In a marital break-up, battles often arise over who will get what property and finances. But the fiercest and most damaging battle is often fought over custody, as if the children were property, too.

In the same way that we insist a wife should never be considered the property of her husband, children are not property. They do not belong to either parent. Their welfare should be paramount to both mother and father. While they ultimately belong to God, in the cycle of earthly events, they belong to themselves. The goal of all good parents, whether the home is intact or broken, should be to prepare their children to take their own place in the future, which belongs to them.

That means the present time, while enormously important, is temporary. It can be compared to crossing the waters of Lake Erie, which is usually a pleasant place to sail. Now and then, however, a wicked storm comes up, the waves and the water turn rough and the winds howl. On these occasions, there is one simple goal: to survive. Somehow you have to make your way safely across the lake and get back to terra firma. When that is accomplished, you can resume your normal course. Stormy times—on lakes and in divorces—are times of transition.

Even at the best of times and the most stable of homes, illness, conflict, insecurity and loneliness can make parenting a challenge. How parents and children respond varies dramatically. Old age, they say, is not for sissies: neither is parenting.

One day in a conversation with my father I was lamenting the difficulty of knowing how to be a good parent. My life as a busy pastor was preventing me from being present when I thought I was needed during this or that problem which one of our children was experiencing. My father smiled at me and said, "Try not to worry about it too much, Rich. No matter what you do, they will grow up anyway."

It stopped me dead in my tracks. It might seem oversimplified when you first hear it, especially if you are a concerned and caring parent, but it helped me keep my own importance out of the way as our children grew up and turned into adults. I learned the lesson well. I have surely passed it along many times to many others. By now our children are adults, and I am happy to write that they are all good friends with Peggy and me.

My father's casual comment addresses one of the most perplexing enigmas in the study of human behavior: whether we become who we are because of our heredity or because of our environment. It is a familiar hitching post for heated discussion. Are we fashioned more by the nature of the genes inside us, or by the nurture we receive from those around us? Do children grow up and take on their own personalities because of who they are, or because of the way their parents treat them? Different studies have produced different answers. The longer I live, the more weight I give to heredity. Our genetic make-up predetermines much of who we are, not only in appearance, but in personality.

In the Cromie family, we use the pronoun "our" to refer to individual family members: "our Cathie," "our Cammie," "our Courtney." We still use the pronoun admiringly with our grandchildren: "our Maddie" and "our Wil." I am not sure who originated the possessive pronoun, but to us, it means we belong together.

If you dropped in on one of our holiday dinners, it would not take long to figure out that a set of highly individual characters are gathered for a festive and noisy meal. We are all so different that we look like the United Nations in recess. We add humbly that our family belongs to God. We try to embody the words from the Book of Joshua, "As for me and my house, we will serve the Lord" (Joshua 24:15). We affirm the importance of parents, grandparents, children and siblings, while at the same time, we are amazed at how different children from the same family home can be.

In an ideal world, good parents are always on the lookout for the well-being of their children. The couple works as a team, sacrificing themselves when necessary to assist the child in building enduring self confidence. It can be a demanding commitment at times: Growing up is difficult. When you catalogue all the possible detriments, it is a wonder that any of us make it at all. Establishing identity and self-esteem is an enormous undertaking. There are a plethora of pressures in our culture to beat us down and wear us out.

It has most likely always been that way. Each generation seems to cherish the distinction of living in the most dangerous time of all. But our current age is filled with options and dangers unknown in the days of yore. In this age of divorce, "our" family is often set aside in the rush to find a pot of gold. For a variety of reasons, families do not tend to "belong" to one another, or to look out for each other the way families did in former times.

The long-range objective of parenthood is to release a child to his or her own cognizance when the time comes that the child is able to manage it. This does not happen suddenly one spring morning. It begins with managing separation along the way. The first day the child goes off to nursery school or kindergarten is an important step in learning to let go. The first overnight slumber party might be another step, as would be the first visit to faraway friends or family. Then comes a Scouting overnight, the move to secondary school, to college, away to miliary service, to a first apartment, out of town for a job. The child gradually learns how to survive on his or her own. Meanwhile, the parents are experiencing growing pains of their own, as I can testify. Proper preparation for each step is necessary for the child to willingly take his or her proper place in the world beyond home and family.

In teaching and counseling, I have long told young parents that there are two basic duties of parenthood. The first is to build up their child's self-esteem, to help them develop self-confidence and to make them feel special. "I am somebody" is more than Psychology 101: It is a shortcut through the woods of advanced theories about what we must do to steady the human ship in the modern maelstrom of change.

The second goal of parenting is to learn when to hold on and when to let go. Some parents hold on too long and stifle the growth of confidence. Children should be released to fend for themselves and to make decisions on their own in progressive stages. This enables them to assume the mantle of responsibility for making their own way through life.

No parent I have ever known is perfect. All have erred by being too cautious or too permissive, sometimes both. Protective parents who are concerned for their children are good folk to have around, but the line of overprotection is easily transgressed and often not recognized in time. As no sensible parent would turn a child loose to cross a busy intersection at age two, no parent should refuse to allow a child to cross the highway to adulthood and independence. Some let go too soon, if they ever held on at all. Too frequently, children are not only forced to cross dangerous street corners on their own, but worse, they grow up with little or no direction at all.

Our special interest here is what happens to children of divorce. Children can be amazingly resilient in surprising ways, but resiliency is not guaranteed. Children in Christian homes with kind, loving, well-intentioned parents can tumble into the valleys of self-rejection, depression, rebellion, addiction and worse. There can be no guarantee that the children of intact homes will fare better than those with separated parents.

Many times they manage to survive, no matter what the challenge. Divorce can be hostile and threatening. Some children manage to overcome it, some do not. Some children seem to be innately able to forge a good result, even from severely hostile environments. Years ago I read Robert Coles, the Harvard and Duke University research psychiatrist, professor and author of a five-volume masterpiece called Children of Crisis. On a more basic level, The Moral Life of Children is sufficient for most people to catch the drift of his discoveries. He found that some children survive against impossible odds, finding useful ways to plow through the adversities of nature and the abuses of man. With no one around to train or guide them, they develop into kind and loving teens and adults, concerned for their fellow human beings. How this happens—how they master unfortunate environments—is mostly a mystery, even to eminent researchers such as Coles.

So how will your children be affected? No one really knows the answer. Over the past 50 years, opinions regarding the way divorce affects children have shifted back-and-forth. I can testify that the literature of the subject is voluminous enough that it would take a lifetime to read and master it all.

At the time I began my ordained ministry, there were few American children from divorced homes. Divorce was a scandal that happened to Hollywood entertainers, not to families down the street. I mentioned earlier that when I was growing up, I was aware of only a few divorced families. My wife recalls no children of divorce in her neighborhood or school.

I suppose it is fair to say that from my limited experience, but also from what I have learned in my work, we thought that children in broken homes were unfortunate victims worthy of pity more than scorn, because their parents did not love them enough to stay together. Their fathers had usually gone away, forcing their mothers to work to support the family. This was the generation before "the latch-key generation," but in a few places no one was at home after school. If the children had no grandmother or neighborly aunt down the block, they were turned out to make it on their own. Obviously, parents were encouraged to patch things up and stay together for sake of the children.

From there I moved to thinking that in some cases it would be better if the couple divorced to spare the children severe conflict and its aftermath in the home. Others joined me in that thinking. As my ministry developed, I came to feel that it was an improvement for children to be out of a quarrelsome home where they would be doomed by the turmoil around them. At least in dovorce, their parents were free to become the people they were meant to be, unencumbered by a marriage they had been forced to enter by pregnancy or fear of being left behind. After all, some had opted for marriage fresh out of school, since everyone was supposed to be married, and the sooner the better. I began to think that freedom would make them better parents, and their children would benefit and thrive.

The problem was that it did not work out that way. The more popular divorce became, the more problems developed. Those were the years when multiple marriages made matters worse. Fear of failure and heartbreak accompanied the change. That caused consternation to those who pleaded for freedom, especially for liberated women.

More recently, opinions have turned around. The number of divorces has fallen, but so has the number of marriages. The two must be viewed side by side. Living together as if married but without a legal stamp of approval, has become acceptable in most areas of the country. Even pregnancy or a new baby no longer requires that the couple marry. In the most privileged of families, unmarried couples rear children with impunity. The dissolution of those unions when they occur is not listed in divorce statistics.

Thankfully, sensible researchers on the topic have come to the fore. I recommend Judith S. Wallerstein, Julia M. Lewis and Sandra Blakeslee's landmark study called The Unexpected Legacy of Divorce, and E. Mavis Hetherington and John Kelly's For Better or For Worse: Divorce Reconsidered. While these books do not agree on some key points, in my opinion both are fair, honest and thorough. Both studies followed a large number of children, some for three decades following the divorce of their parents.

Wallerstein, et al, argue that the unexpected legacy from the multitude of divorces has placed more pressure on children. Their struggles in broken homes are more difficult than most imagine. She says these children-now-adults have not fared as well as we thought they would. As they mature, they tend to have trouble forming and keeping enduring relationships. They are more suspicious of marital commitment as a lifelong endeavor. Their divorce rates are nearly double those from homes where there had been no divorce. They tend to have deeper emotional, psychological and social problems. Their use of drugs and alcohol tends to be higher. I use the word "tend," because the authors refuse to generalize. Individual stories and interviews are the medium of the message.

Hetherington and Kelly are more optimistic. They state that 75 percent of the children-turned-adults studied tended to survive reasonably well in the long run. Almost every child has adjustment problems at the beginning of a divorce. Their book argues that if the remaining 25 percent continue to have some social and psychological problems, that should be compared with the 10 percent from intact marriages and homes that have the same or similar problems. The authors admit that divorce is a high-risk venture, but that it is often necessary when the alternatives of violence and abuse are considered.

For Christians, there is special interest in the religious and moral development of children whose parents have been divorced. Once again, generalizations cannot be made. It depends on the child, the parents and the circumstances. What we can say with some certainty is that children of divorce seem to be less successful in adapting favorably to religious and moral issues. Conversely, some children of divorce seem to draw closer to their churches and young people's religious societies, perhaps out of the need for developing social relationships or to have a second home.

Some researchers note that children of divorce seem morally adrift. I mentioned earlier their inability to commit to an enduring marriage and the increased likelihood of their being divorced. It also seems that fewer attend worship on a regular basis. There are many variables of age and location and other circumstances. More research into the religious involvements of children is necessary, but only a small minority of those who write on this topic would say that children from divorced homes are doomed to live inferior lives. It could be that they have fewer possibilities for a normal existence, but that opinion is still in the making.

Let me suggest some additional reading for interested

parents. I was impressed with a book by Dr. Isolina Ricci called, Mom's House, Dad's House: Making Two Homes for Your Child. The book abounds with useful observations on procedures to follow when joint custody is agreed on. Sharing separate homes with each parent is becoming a more popular way to nurture children following divorce. I found the References and Resources section at the end of the book to be a veritable treasure trove of good things to do and read.

Late in my research I came across a new book by Elizabeth Marquardt entitled, Between Two Worlds: The Inner Lives of Children of Divorce. Marquardt studied 1,500 children from homes in which divorce intruded. She found children of divorce are two to three times more likely to have serious social and emotional problems in adulthood, and that by being forced to become adults before their time, they also miss out on a lot of their childhood.

To summarize: There can be no doubt that divorce makes an important impact on the lives of children. No one knows for sure what specific direction any particular child will take. However, their ability to manage the future is related to how their parents manage the divorce.

Growing up in a separated family obviously shapes a child's life. But thoughtful parents can become the potters who help to mold the clay. If they do it with self-sacrifice and love, they are more likely to have a well-loved, self-respecting child who thrives in adulthood. Good parenthood is always based on self-sacrifice. Divorced parents who work together to make their parenthood a priority can manage just about as well as couples in happy homes. A child needs to feel secure and loved. Those who are made to feel special are more likely to make it through with gusto and grace.

The first prerequisite in guiding the lives of your children is to make sure you have custody of you. This way, you will have sufficient energy and interest to devote to parenting. If you are strong and confident, you will be able to share the journey successfully with your children. Watch out for them: They are the greatest gift God ever gives.

CHAPTER 10
SEX AND THE SINGLE CHRISTIAN

This chapter begins long ago and far away. In the early 1960s, I taught a Presbyterian Communicants' Class at our church, a year long exercise of preparing 30 or so 8th grade students for church membership. It was arduous. The day for the final examination by the elders arrived. Admittedly, it was partly a charade. I had prepped the students for the kinds of questions the church session might ask. I had also slipped some questions to a few of the elders. The show went on. The communicants were exemplary. The session was impressed. The senior pastor was puffed up.

Basking in reflected glory, he decided to put his own spin on the gathering. With a ministerial chuckle he leaned out over the lectern and said to the class, "I am proud of you. Now, I want to know if you have any questions for the elders. I am sure they can answer them." I suppose he assumed they would ask how many sacraments we had, how many books were in the Bible, or the other names of Shadrach, Meshach and Abednego, a popular ecclesiastical trivia question at the time.

Now imagine a class of 12- and 13-year-olds, a trifle nervous on their big day, but so newly trained they could have slam-dunked the elders with ease, thinking what to ask. I was a little nervous too, thinking of all that might be coming. At best it could have been awkward for the elders. At worst, it could have flopped.

A peculiar thing happened. The chapel fell silent. Undaunted, the pastor egged them on. Finally, one student at the end of the second row raised his hand half way up, and asked: "Sir, I would like to know…if I want to be a good Christian…is it a sin … to want to see…. a woman … naked?" Almost all the elders laughed. Some of his fellow students snickered. The senior pastor almost had a heart attack. He motioned for me to end the exam and hurried on to the required motions and closing prayer. The meeting was over. I walked out with the boy.

I was puzzled and a little depressed. I had treated the students to an extended course of instruction, sharing what it meant to be a Christian. I had introduced them to the articles of faith, the rudimentary meaning of the Bible, and the need to commit themselves to Christ. I had shared a host of practical suggestions on how to live the Christian life. It had been a good course.

But I had missed the number one question on the mind of that young man, and I would guess, on the minds of most other students in the class. They were entering adolescence, a volcanic time of transition. Their number one concern was the overwhelming new demand and presence of sex. The sine qua non of their existence was how to manage this rising new visitor who was revising their ability to relate to themselves and to those of the opposite sex.

We would have done as well to teach them how many angels could dance on the head of a pin. In the middle ages, that was a major objective of the class for confirmands. Our oversight of their personal problems echoed a shortcoming the church failed to cover through the centuries and that lingers on in our modern world: we fail to meet people's contemporary needs. We answer questions no one is asking. Is it any wonder that young people have left the traditional churches in droves? And, not only the young.

The unique demands of sex do not end with a puzzled 13-year-old. It prances through the teenage years into adulthood. It wanders through the middle years. It can be consuming, and with some, it never seems to end. In recent years, with advances in treatment and with stimulating drugs, it has dramatically returned as an issue with mature couples, and continues with some who have grown older. It should not surprise you that men in their retirement years still ponder over sexual feelings and needs with their pastors and friends. I talked with a young woman some time ago who was astonished when she discovered that her grandfather kept his interest in sex to the very end of his life.

As pastor I have always tried to speak openly about sexuality with young and old alike. The subject comes up each time I speak with couples in premarital counseling. It remains a vital issue long after the wedding day. It tops the list of marital problems. It is the beginning and the end of infidelities. It is present in unwanted pregnancies. It drives the conversations when couples deliberate whether to live together before marriage. It is the persistent doubt of those who never married. It is a concern of men and women who decide to live together without marriage. It is a major part of the lifestyle choice for gays and lesbians. It should be part of every church curriculum.

And it surely belongs in a book for those who are

divorced. God made us with sexual treasures and desires. They do not subside when we marry, and they do not disappear when we are divorced. Rather, as many have confided to me, if the marriage has included good sexual activity, and it often does even when other conflicts are present, the loss of that excitement and release is missed all the more.

In polite Christian circles we often shy away from such open conversation. Yet the Bible is not squeamish or reticent at all. Sex appears there as often as prayer or faith or stewardship. It took root in the Garden of Eden. After the first couple disobeyed the Creator and took the luscious fruit of the forbidden tree, they realized they were naked and clothed themselves with fig leaves.

Later, when the Nephilim, the sons of God, saw that the young women of the earth were fair, they came down and "took wives for themselves and all that they chose." It sounds more like Greek mythology, but it reads: "The sons of God went into the daughters of humans, who bore children to them. These were the heroes of old, warriors of renown" (Genesis 6:1-4). Notice that this incident is written as a statement of fact, without apology or explanation, and without a hint of reprobation. Not that it was literally true, but the author did not condemn the intermingling.

The Bible continues to discuss sexual attraction and its aftermath: eighteen centuries before Christ, Abraham tried to pass his wife off as his sister so that Pharaoh could have sex with her and would not have to kill Abraham to get to her (Genesis 12:10f).

Later, when Abraham's wife Sarah was barren, she gave her Egyptian slave-girl, Hagar, to Abraham, who "went into her and Hagar conceived" (Genesis 16:3f). The son born to this union was Ishmael. The tradition of Islam holds that Mohammed and all Arab Muslims are descended from him. Sarah later became jealous of Hagar's lusty fertility and of her personal success with Abraham, and she drove Hagar out into the desert.

Genesis 29 tells how Jacob came to marry two sisters, Leah and Rachel, at the same time. He deeply loved Rachel, but on the appointed wedding night, Laban sent his elder daughter into the marriage tent in place of Rachel, to Jacob's horror in the morning. His father-in-law agreed to give him Rachel as a second wife if he worked his farm for seven more years.

There is no hint that the double wedding was wrong. Laban's deceitful action caused the groom's ire. When Leah produced three sons in a row, Rachel was naturally jealous, and being without child, she gave her maid, Bilhah, to Jacob, presumably out of her love for her husband and her desire to have a child. Jacob and Bilhah slept together often enough that two sons were born to their union.

I remind you that the total 12 sons of Jacob became the 12 vaunted leaders of the 12 Tribes of Israel, whose names are inscribed on the 12 gates of the New Heaven in Revelation 21. Hardly a routine family, this is a robust and vibrant assemblage of wives and concubines whose sons all have Jacob as their father. The co-mingled family is introduced without moral commentary and without moral condemnation.

A couple of centuries later, an officer of the Pharaoh of Egypt named Potiphar had a lovely wife, who took a personal interest in Joseph, a son of Jacob who had been sold into Egyptian slavery by his brothers. When Joseph refused to lie with her, she tore the shirt off his back, took it to her husband and told him that Joseph had tried to molest her. Joseph ended up in jail. The story has a happy ending, for Joseph was later released and became the Prime Minister of Egypt. The Bible says that while his brothers intended it for evil, God intended it for good.

Later, the story of Samson in the Book of Judges reads more like a modern tabloid than the ancient Word of God. He fell in love with a Philistine woman, to the horror of his Jewish parents. Things did not go well at the wedding and reception, so Samson left in a huff. When he returned to take his bride, he found that she had already been given to his best man. He got angry again. On the way home, he visited a prostitute in Gaza and "went into her." He later fell for a comely lass named Delilah from the Valley of Sorek. That was his downfall. She enticed him, then she betrayed him to the Philistines. He, and many of them, lost their lives. Samson is an honored judge, a man of God, and yet all his troubles started when his sexual proclivities took command (Judges 13-14).

The commandments and punishments regarding sexual activity listed in the laws of the Pentateuch, especially Leviticus and Deuteronomy, are fascinating, brutally honest, and at times, astonishing. An endless variety of sexual deeds are exposed there, with an exhausting list of admonishments and advice. Adultery and fornication are paramount. Masturbation does not go unnoticed, nor does incest. Penalties for a young woman who claims she was raped out in the country are different from one who claims she was raped in the city. Presumably someone would have heard and rescued her if she had been accosted inside the city gates. If a man had sexual relations with a slave, it was a minor infraction. If he had sex with the wife of another Israelite, both of them were to be put to death. Homosexuality is not overlooked. Two of the 10 Commandments directly concern sexual acts: "You shall not commit adultery; and you shall not covet your neighbor's wife" (Exodus 20). It goes on to say that your neighbor's female servant should not be coveted either, not because she should remain inviolate, but because she belongs to the neighbor.

Later in the Book of II Samuel, it says that as King David was walking about on the roof of his palace enjoying the view of the lovely hills and valleys, he spied a comely young woman bathing at the house next to his (II Samuel 11). David sent for her and wooed her. Who could resist a king? They "knew" each other (What a lovely description of the sexual union!). Not long after, Bathsheba told David she was pregnant. David moved Uriah, her soldier husband, up to the front battle lines, where he was killed. David, as he often did, took the beautiful young lady for his wife. Years later it says that David pleased God in all things, "except in this matter of Uriah" (I Kings 15:5). That seems to mean that his mortal sin was not stealing Bathsheba from her husband, not the adulterous act itself, but of sending Uriah to his death.

In the history of Susanna found in the Apocrypha (an addition to the Book of Daniel), the lovely young Susanna was bathing alone in her father's garden. Two stalwart elders, who visited her father each day on religious business, became enamored and were finally "overwhelmed with passion for her." One day they hid themselves in the garden. When she dismissed her maids and undressed, they ran to her and said they were in love with her, and that if she did not consent to frolic with them, they would tell everyone that they found her in the garden with a young man. Being a woman of virtue, she refused them anyway. It is a longer story, but in the end they were convicted by Daniel of bearing false witness. The poor girl had been accosted by the original "dirty old men."

The New Testament is not as graphic and dramatic as the Old Testament, but the interest in the sexuality of men and women does not abate. For example, Joseph was ready to break his engagement to Mary, a virgin, when he discovered that she was pregnant. He was sure some other man had visited her. He was wrong, of course; the Holy Spirit had come upon her (Matthew 1:18-25).

In John 4, our Lord offered a drink of water to a Samaritan woman at the well. She had been married five times and was currently living with a man who was not her husband. She was amazed when Jesus knew all about her. But, he did not condemn her, and she left with a question in her heart.

Four chapters later, the authorities were about to stone a woman to death because she had been caught in the act of adultery. It sounds like "cruel and unusual punishment" to us. In our day, we would expect her husband to file for divorce, and both could go on to marry someone else. With the elders standing there, Jesus said "Whoever of you has no sin, let him cast the first stone." They dropped their rocks and went quietly away. Neither did he condemn her. Instead, he said, "Go and sin no more."

In I Corinthians, St. Paul complained that one of the Christian young men was sleeping with his father's second wife. He was also concerned that young women should marry quickly, lest they go astray. He added that men should marry if they were tempted to have sex. In his letters, he wrote that wives and husbands were required to make themselves available to each other. It was not always on his mind, but it was often in the forefront of his Epistles.

The Bible leaves few sexual stones unturned. Rape is frequently mentioned. Fornication and adultery are both condemned. Sodomy, in its variations, is anathema to the people of God. Homosexuality appears from time to time. Sex among the elderly is also there. Sarah got scolded for laughing when God said she would soon have a son, but she had one. Sarah referred to the sexual union as "pleasurable." The judgments on those who deviated from the current laws were usually severe.

My point in mentioning this recitation of sexual behavior is to indicate that all of the above were present in daily life in Biblical times. We have no exclusive on sexual problems and deviations in our time.

In the larger Biblical view, sex is a treasured gift to be used for procreation and for enjoyment. It is also a powerful and dangerous force. Above all, the topic should never be ignored. It belongs in the center of who we are and what we believe.

———— • ————

Let me move on to what the Bible says about sex and the single Christian. A cursory background summary is all we can manage here (I plan to publish a more detailed study in the future). Biblical teaching is not always as clear and final as we are led by some to believe.

In the New Testament, believers are exhorted to avoid "porneia," which is translated as fornication, unchastity, adultery and immorality of many kinds. When the sexual relationship goes into forbidden territory, it is condemned. What that exact boundaries are, however, can be subject to disagreement among believers. The writers of the 66 Bible books could not have foreseen the complexities and nuances prevalent in the 21st century. When they do touch on specific areas of interest to us, the meaning can often be ambiguous.

The Epistles of the New Testament seem to teach that all sex outside the married relationship of a man and a woman is sin and should be avoided. In the Gospels, however, those who depart from that guideline seem not to be guilty of felonious crimes, or even of serious misdemeanors. Jesus forgave them. Once forgiven, they return to the routine of their daily lives. In the Old Testament, which we believe is also the Word of God, conclusions are offered for a wide variety of sexual situations, but some of them are in conflict as well.

The ancient Bible lives on and on, but it also adapts itself to the interpretation of each new generation. It is the Eternal Word of God, but it was written by and for God's people who were immersed in the problems and possibilities of their own daily lives. Since its adoption as official canon, the Bible has been reinterpreted and reapplied to the issues of each passing era.

By the way, the canon of our 66 books, although officially adopted earlier by a Church Council, did not find universal acceptance until after the Reformation of the Sixteenth Century. Martin Luther did not agree that all 27 New Testament books belong in the Bible. Further, interpretations of what the Scriptures meant varied widely. Some conclusions John Calvin reached from the Bible and put into practice in Geneva seem alien to our way of life. In some ways it was a repressive society. The rules for private behavior were strict and universally intrusive. Failure to arrive at worship, for example, was a civil offense. Proven heresy was a capital offense.

Later in the United States, the authorities in 18th century Salem, Massachusetts who used the Bible to torture and execute witches now seem malicious and evil to us. Throughout the ages, but especially in the span of my lifetime, the rigid assumptions of a previous time thought to be self-evident have been revised by common consent of God's people.

Some object to my way of thinking, calling it self-serving. Tinkering with what the Bible says leads to poor theology, they say. But it is not only in matters of sex that our understanding has changed.

Let me suggest a parallel to what the Bible says about the role of women in the church. Many customs and commands of the Old Testament and some of the New Testament teachings of St. Paul deny the equality of women in the home, society and especially in church leadership. When I was ordained, I knew what the Bible said, but I still believed that women belonged equally in the circle of ordained leaders. At the start, I honed up my exegetical and debating skills and tried to prove that St. Paul did not really mean to deny the equality of women in church leadership. I preached that the apparent bias was a misunderstanding of what he said and meant.

Granted that trying to restate what St. Paul wrote on this matter was a tremendous task and at best, a tenuous conclusion. The Epistles seem to be clear about what a woman can and cannot do in the church. I Corinthians 7 describes the secondary role of women. It is expanded in places such as Ephesians 5 and I Peter 3. I Timothy 2 gives more detail:

"Let a woman learn in silence with full submission. I permit no woman to teach or to have authority over a man; she is to keep silent." It reaches its zenith in I Corinthians 14:34 ff: "Women should be silent in the churches. For they are not permitted to speak, but should be subordinate, as the law also says. If there is anything they desire to know, let them ask their husbands at home. For it is shameful for a woman to speak in church."

There are few sensible Christians who would want to be part of a church where practices based on these verses were in force.

The church has felt led to modify what appear to be literal directives of the Scripture in keeping with the guidance we have received from the Living Christ and the Holy Spirit. God speaks in and through the pages of the Bible. He also speaks to us beyond and above them, as the Spirit guides our understanding.

The Bible is not a Paper Pope. We are not commanded to lift certain words and phrases off the page and make rigid applications in the 21st century. Some customs proscribed in the early life of God's people would alter our lifestyle considerably. For example, the Old Testament forbids eating pork, yet it is nice to enjoy a pork barbeque sandwich once in a while without feeling guilty. I like to see women dressed for church with a string of pearls, gold rings, bracelets and necklaces, even if I know such ostentation is specifically forbidden in I Timothy 2:9.

The Bible also has teachings regarding sexual situations and the right to file for divorce. What the Scripture says should not be ignored. However, we need to adapt and apply what it meant in the time it was written to our own situation.

I do not want you to conclude that I claim authority to interpret the Scriptures however I choose. My point is that we can acknowledge what the Bible says; but in the presence of God, we can move forward to an analysis of what we are required to do in the here and now. In some cases we might choose to disagree with what the Bible seems to say. Those times are few and far between and they should be handled gently and in deep humility.

Critics of this approach tell me this attitude endangers the inspiration and the infallibility of the Scriptures, and that my "compromise" makes it easier to believe whatever we choose. They say it releases me to counsel others to follow their own evolving conscience. But in fact, searching for that compromise between the Eternal Law of God and the reigning practice of the time makes the Bible and my daily decisions much more difficult.

Rather, it forces me to wrestle with the words of Scripture as they are handed down, but also to look to the meaning of the Biblical commandments in the time they were written, knowing what they meant to those who first heard them. Then they can become the Word of God to me.

Thankfully, I am not alone. In the end, it is a matter of how you believe God works with his people. God offers us the Scriptures to be sure, but they are not wedded to the past. God is always on the move. We are challenged to follow where the Lord God leads, not where the ancient writers stopped. Our goal is to listen for a current command, as we synthesize the words and meanings of Scripture with the presence of the Holy Spirit to guide us in this century.

There are other issues that call for similar explanations and even exemptions. At one time, church fathers argued that the Bible condoned slavery. Ephesians advised us that slaves should be obedient to their masters (Ephesians 6:5f). Titus 2:9 adds that slaves should not only be submissive, "but they are not to talk back to their masters, and they are to show complete and perfect fidelity." For a couple of centuries, sane and believing clergymen, lay leaders and plantation owners in this country tried to use those selected verses to keep their slaves in line.

There are other commandments and laws from the Bible that the community of Christ's people has chosen to rephrase through the passing generations. The variety of dietary laws in the Pentateuch seem archaic to us today. The directives concerning lepers, or the rules governing women during their monthly cycles, or the law requiring a man to marry his deceased brother's widow, or commands against eating rabbit, for example. Although these matters appear as laws of God, time and experience give us leave to qualify their importance. The Bible must become a judge against itself. If the entire Bible is the Word of God; if the words of its English translation were dictated by the Lord God Almighty and eternally inerrant; if people of every era who patterned their behavior on what they were told The Bible means, then Christians of all the ages will have a lot of answering to do for a myriad of sins which they committed unwittingly.

114

Concerning sex and the single Christian, a reconsideration of permissible behavior has been underway for a long time, having peaked in the last 50 years. We have witnessed a shift in moral authority from the laws of the church and state to the individual Christian's God-given right to decide. That shift seems to me to have some merit. This is not to say that every change in our interpretation of God's Word is an improvement. We need the anchor and advice of the Scriptures to help us navigate through the stormy moral times in which we live. Matters of experimental marriages, casually available sex, fathers (and mothers) who abandon family, abortion for convenience, widespread pornography, and all the rest, have done great harm to our society, especially to women and children. The question, "Where does that leave me in the choices I have to make?" is a valid one.

Let me offer some suggestions: The first thing I say is that you should not try to shift gears too quickly. Sexual involvement for single and divorced persons takes you into deep water. It reaches to the innermost core of who you are. It creates some dangerous moral, spiritual and personal problems. I caution you to walk slowly into this new terrain.

I have counseled many who have dealt carelessly with sexual intimacy. As a result, their lives and confidence were forever changed and damaged. During transitions, people become vulnerable. If you feel that experimenting with sex is wrong, be firm in your opinion and let everybody know. The winds of change blow erratically. A friend of mine once said, "It is hard to live in a draft. You never know when it will come around again and blow you away."

How then, do we decide? The synthesis comes when I return to the message of this book: You must have custody of you. If you have taken responsibility for your own life; if you have freed yourself from inner feelings of guilt; if you have found the right culprit in your divorce and dealt with it; if you believe that God can and will guide you even if you decide to depart from the roads you traveled yesterday; if you have the courage to step out on your own and with eyes wide open, opt for increasing intimacy outside of marriage; then you are free to decide what you want to do. Go for it. As one friend told me years ago, "I am a 38-year-old single, divorced woman, not a teenage virgin. What could possibly be wrong with me having a good time with a man I enjoy?"

Well, other than advising her to be cautious and reminding her that pregnancy is still possible; other than some fatherly advice against giving her heart away too soon; other than some explicit warnings about venereal diseases and the need for proper protection; and with an offer to discuss what the Bible says about sex and the single person (which she refused), I sent her on her way with a silent prayer that God would protect her, and he did.

I also knew a Christian woman from New Jersey who had been married for almost 20 years. Sadly, her husband suffered a horrible stroke, which left him nearly comatose. The nursing home staff had a full-time job just keeping him alive. For three years she visited him every day. She sat there intermittently crying, reading and saying her prayers. Then she would go home and cry some more.

She was at the end of her tether when she came to me one day for advice. "Does God expect me to live like this for the next 20 years?" she asked. "I know I promised to be faithful in sickness and in health, but what do I do now? My friends all have families. They take wonderful vacations.

They enjoy life. I'm lonely. Am I supposed to sit and look at the walls? I have found a very nice friend who wants to take me to dinner and talk. Should I go? What does the Lord God want me to do?"

What would you have said if you had been her pastor? You might be surprised to learn that I told her that she was entitled to a life of her own. After all, Jesus came to bring us the abundant life (John 10:10). I doubt he meant we were supposed to endure loneliness and isolation while we wait for time to come to our rescue. She listened, cried and thanked me. Shortly after, she decided to spend some time with her new friend. Her life became more complicated as the relationship deepened, but it also became much more rewarding and exciting. I was proud of her faith and sensitivity. I am sure that her willingness to step out in courage, calling on her inner strength to do what was right, received the blessing of the Lord.

My comments in this section are obviously intended for mature Christian adults. They do not apply equally to unmarried teens who are involved in the process of setting their own standards for personal behavior. Their developing passage is a special time that requires another approach and attitude.

I repeat, be careful. Casual sex can be sinful and degrading. It is also dangerous and often dumb. With disease, possible pregnancy and trivial exploitation, the intimacy for which we were made can go astray so easily. Don Juan may look like a good lover, but he makes a lousy friend. Don't give you heart away too soon. God gave you ribs to protect it. When two become one, it should be a spiritual occasion. The King James translation says that Adam "knew" Eve and they became one flesh. That seems to me to be the essential story.

By choice or by chance, some couples are not concerned with sexual intercourse per se. There are of course other ways for consenting adults to find release and enjoyment without some of the risks. As we grow older, or have surgeries of one kind or another, the ability to have complete intimacy in intercourse becomes difficult, if not impossible.

Although there are alternate approaches to pleasure, I have been told that feelings of guilt, the specter of betraying a spouse long gone, or the lingering inner voice of some dominant parent, pastor or teacher can intrude and hamper one's enjoyment. Guilt has a power all its own.

When those feelings have been overcome and you decide to move forward, the same notes of caution apply: Move slowly, be kind and loving, listen to your partner, relax and work through the discrepancies. Live your life in the present. Put guilt away and let it rest in peace. Be adult enough to claim the joy you have today and look forward to tomorrow. You only go around this mortal life once. Take custody of you!

A young widow in a new dating relationship once asked me if I thought sex outside of marriage was a sin. I said I thought that it probably was. At times the Bible echoes that warning. But I went on to say it was probably also a sin to refuse the joy that life can bring, sinful to have to endure solitude, sinful to set aside the reawakening of physical pleasures and sinful to prevent a person you love from sharing your life and happiness.

Life is not as simple as it used to be. Sometimes progress makes me sad. There is a surfeit of sex all around us. The dangers to young people are especially huge. The risks are great, and the resources to deal with inner conflicts are more difficult to find.

I wish the world were different. I wish everyone who wanted to have a nice wife, a loving husband, some true friends and, like in Lake Wobegon, wonderfully behaved children, would have their way most all of the time. I wish no one would have to be alone or be abused or feel that life was worthless. I wish there were no rapists, no drunken drivers, no murderers, no poverty, no suicides, no prejudice and no child abusers. I wish everyone had a father and mother as kind and caring as mine. I wish all children had mothers completely devoted to them, as my wife is to our three daughters. I wish no one would have deviant sexual attractions. I wish no adult would ever sexually abuse a child. I wish the original couple had never been forced out of the Garden of Eden. But Eden is long gone, and heaven is not yet here. We must live, as theologian Karl Barth said, "Between the times."

I wish no married person would ever have the urge to risk unfaithfulness. I wish no wife or husband would ever let the other down. I wish that divorce would never be an issue. I wish neither partner would get so involved with his or her own life and forget the needs of the other. I wish everyone were perfect. But since Adam and Eve took the fruit off the tree, humankind has been drifting farther away from perfection.

There are a myriad of other problems in the world more worrisome than what two adult people decide to do in their private sexual lives: War and prejudice and abuse and alcohol and drugs and rape and wind and fire and earthquakes and poverty and prejudice and starving children and drunken drivers and hunger and homelessness and children's rights and abominable prisons and ghettos of hopelessness which stalk the lives of God's children every day and night, to name a few.

With all that in the larger picture, it is difficult for me to get overly concerned about an adult single divorced person choosing to spend some tender moments with another adult. If they knowingly want to claim some joy in sharing life to the fullest with each other, I understand. What is more, I think the Lord does also. There are caution flags flying all the way down the highway. There are necessary ground rules to be mutually agreed on and followed religiously.

True, it is a risk. But I would rather see 20 moments shared in love, than 20 years of a sad, unfulfilling marriage. I would rather hear 100 words of kindness outside a marriage than 10,000 unkind words within. I would rather have a man and a woman work things out together in love than listen to 2,000 married couples screaming at each other, or maybe worse, abandoning their marriages to silence and boredom for days and decades to come.

Some would say that makes it all relative. Situational ethics were in vogue 30-40 years ago. They taught that the situation, not the rules or commandments, sets the framework for moral decisions. I do not subscribe to that. It would move us out of the ethical realm completely and make every choice relative to what a person feels at the moment. It implies that moral decisions depend on situational longings, and that can be an excuse for self- indulgent irresponsibility.

I prefer to say that while our Christian decisions occur in the particular time and place, which in God's time we find ourselves, we are still obliged to look to the Biblical teaching and the tradition of the Church for its teachings. We also seek prayerful guidance from the Living God, who interacts with us today as he did with believers of old. In both cases, followers of the Lord are called on to act in love and kindness for the other person. If given a choice, we should always opt for kindness and honesty in human relationships, not because every other prompting is wrong and irrelevant, but because kindness and love and honesty are better.

The fruit of the Spirit is love, joy, peace, patience, kindness, generosity, faithfulness, gentleness and self-control (Galatians 5:22ff). Be bound to those in Jesus Christ and have the courage to claim a life of joy. There is no perfect choice; there is no perfect life except the one to come in eternity. In between, that leaves us to opt for the best choice available.

CONCLUSION

So much more could be written regarding Christian marriage and divorce. However, I have covered the purpose I had in mind for this book. I add a few concluding comments on where we have been.

We began by sketching some changing attitudes on marriage and divorce in recent decades. When I was ordained, divorce within the church was seen as an unforgivable sin and a disgrace. Divorced Christians were treated as failures. A clergyman whose marriage broke up was removed from his pulpit and given his walking papers. In recent years, the stigma of divorce has been softened or removed.

We turned next to the Bible and examined what it says about marriage and divorce. We challenged the reigning conclusion that God's purpose in creating man and woman was that they should marry and remain married to each other for the remainder of their lives. The Bible does not say or even imply that. Other lifestyles are followed by the people of God all throughout the Old and New Testaments.

As we moved through the Scriptures, we looked at the variety of relationships men and women had with each other. In the New Testament, we looked at what Jesus taught about marriage, divorce and remarriage, concluding that the traditional view prohibiting the Christian blessing of marriage to someone who has been divorced needs to be re-examined.

We then moved ahead to the present. Our first concern was for those who were considering divorce. We encouraged them to take a last look around. The changing ethos regarding marriage these days can permit a couple to end their marriage in haste. A good evaluation of the strength of a marriage, as well as its difficulties, is a good investment of time, energy and professional help.

But that good look around causes many to conclude that the time for divorce has come. It is useful to have the necessary background to make that decision. This book tries to offer some of that, as well as what to do in the most pressing of problems.

We moved on to those who have been divorced and discussed the aftershocks. The decision to separate can be painful and depressing. It is often a perilous journey, especially for the one on whom the divorce has been forced. But both former partners are affected by a wide range of emotions. Whether guilty, innocent or both, rigorous readjustments are needed. The road to recovery is rugged and steep, but we have a wonderful Guide and God to help us up.

We then introduced a series of specific pitfalls that must be circumvented in order for recovery to be successful. Helping children adjust is particularly critical. All the evidence is not yet in about how divorce affects young children, but the love of their parents surely helps them on their way to a good and happy life.

Teaching yourself how to handle feelings of guilt and self-pity and anger and loneliness are slow moving but essential maneuvers. Finally, learning to forgive yourself and your former spouse gives you freedom to move on.

In the last chapter we examined the personal issue of sex. There are many Christians who will disagree with these conclusions. But what a healthy adult Christian, who desires to give and receive the love and affection of another is expected to do and not do, is worth an open and honest look.

I think of the young woman who came to me in tears one day to tell me that her husband had left her for a woman down at the office. The wife had been complaining to her friends and support group for months about how thoughtless her husband was and how he forced her to live in his shadow. She asked what she was supposed to do now that he had gone and she was alone. I said I could not tell her what to do, but with all that had stifled her in their marriage, surely the time for divorce had come. "You are free to become the woman you always planned to be. Now, go and do it. Take custody of yourself!" I told her.

I am happy to tell you that she did.

BIBLIOGRAPHY AND SUGGESTED READING

Adams, Jay E. *Marriage, Divorce, Remarriage in the Bible.* Zondervan Publishing House, Grand Rapids MI, 1980.

Barth, Karl. *Church Dogmatics; Volume III, Doctrine of Creation.* T &T Clark, Edinburgh, Scotland, 1961.

Clapp, Genevieve. *Divorce & New Beginnings: A Complete Guide to Recovery, Solo Parenting, Co-parenting, and Stepfamilies.* John Wiley and Sons, Inc. New York, NY, second edition, 1999.

Eldredge, Robert Sr. *Can Divorced Christians Remarry?* Choice Publications, Camarillo, CA, 2002.

Ellison, Stanley A. *Divorce and Remarriage in the Church,* revised and enlarged edition. Zondervan Publishing House, Grand Rapids MI, 1980.

Fisher, Bruce and Albert, Robert. *Rebuilding: When Your Relationship Ends.* Impact Publishers, Atascadero, CA, 2002.

Fisher, Helen E. *Anatomy of Love: The Natural History of Monogamy, Adultery, and Divorce.* W. W. Norton & Co., NY, 1992.

Ford, Debbie. *Spiritual Divorce.* Harper Publishers, San Francisco, 2001.

Hailey, Elizabeth. *Joanna's Husband and David's Wife.* Delacorte Press, New York, 1986.

Hetherington, E. Mavis and Kelly, John. *For Better or For Worse: Divorce Reconsidered.* W. W. Morton & Co., NY, 2002

Instone-Brewer, David. *Divorce and Remarriage in the Bible: The Social and Literary Context.* William B. Eerdmans Publishing Co., Grand Rapids, MI, 2002.

Instone-Brewer, David. *Divorce and Remarriage in the First and Twenty First Century.* Grove Books, Ltd. Cambridge, UK, 2001.

Keener, Craig S. *And Marries Another: Divorce and Remarriage in the Teaching of the New Testament.* Hendrickson Publishing, Peabody, MA, 1991.

Kipnis, Laura. *Against Love: A Polemic.* Pantheon Books, NY, 2003.

Kitchen, S. B. *A History of Divorce.* The Lawbook Exchange, Ltd., Union, NJ, 2002.

Krantzler, Mel and Krantzler, Pat. *The New Creative Divorce.* Adams Media Corporation, Holbrook, MA, 1998.

Marquardt, Elizabeth. *Between Two Worlds: The Inner Lives of Children of Divorce.* Crown Publishers, New York, 2005.

McRoberts, Darlene. *Second Marriage: The Promise and the Challenge.* Augsburg Publishing House, MN, 1978.

McVeigh, Kate. *Single and Loving It.* Harrison House, Tulsa, OK, 2003.

McWade, Micki. *Getting Up, Getting Over, Getting On: A Twelve Step Guide to Divorce Recovery.* Champion Press, Ltd., Beverly Hills, CA, 1999.

Missildine, W. Hugh. *Your Inner Child of the Past.* Simon and Schuster, New York, 1963

Monroe, Myles. *Single, Married, Separated, and Life after Divorce.* Destiny Image Publishers, Inc., Shippensburg, PA, 2003.

Moseley, Doug and Moseley, Naomi. *Making Your Second Marriage a First Class Success.* Prima Publishing, Roseville, CA, 1998.

Phillips, Roderick. *Untying the Knot: A Short History of Divorce.* Cambridge University Press, Cambridge, UK, 1991.

Phipps, William E. *Was Jesus Married?* Harper Row, New York 1970

Ricci, Isolina. *Mom's House, Dad's House, Making Two Homes for Your Child.* Simon and Shuster, NY, 1997.

Richardson, Cheryl. *Take Time For Your Life.* Broadway Books, NY, 1998.

Smoke, Jim. *Growing Through Divorce.* Harvest House Publishers, Eugene, OR, revised, updated edition, 1995.

Trafford, Abigail. *Crazy Time – Surviving Divorce.* Harper and Row, NY, 1982.

Wallerstein, Judith S. and Blakeslee, Sandra. *Second Chances: Men, Women and Children a Decade After Divorce.* Ticknor & Fields Publishing, NY, 1990.

Wallerstein, Judith S., Lewis, Julia and Blakeslee, Sandra. *The Unexpected Legacy of Divorce: A 25 Year Landmark Study.* Hyperion Publishing, NY, 2000.

Whitehead, Barbara Dafoe. *The Divorce Culture.* Vintage Books, New York, 1998.

Wilson, James Q. *The Marriage Problem: How Our Culture Has Weakened Families.* Harper Collins Publishers, NY, 2002.

Woodrow, Ralph Edward. *Divorce and Remarriage: What Does The Bible Say?* Evangelistic Association, Riverside, CA, 1982.

The Holy Bible, Revised Standard Version, World Wide Publishers, 1971.

Our purpose is to bring the living water of Jesus Christ to the various "deserts" of human life. We provide books, tapes and encouragement for clergy and laity. Current publications include *When You Lose Someone You Love, When a Child Dies, Christ Will See You Through, When Alzheimer's Disease Strikes, A Journey Through Cancer, When Your Life Includes a Wheelchair,* and more.

We will gladly send a selection of our books and booklets without charge, including a brochure that describes them. For more information, please see www.desmin.org.

If you would like additional copies of this book, please contact us at:

Desert Ministries, Inc.
P. O. 747
Matthews, NC 28106

Phone:..........704/849-0901
Fax: 704/845-1502
Web site: ......www.Desmin.org